Minnesota

OFF THE BEATEN PATH™

"A county-by-county exploration of the most interesting offbeat things to see in the state."
—*Travel & Leisure*

"An engaging book."
—*Family Travel Times*

"Lists more than 150 sites and attractions."
—*Minneapolis Star Tribune*

"Many engaging places and events that add to Minnesota's unique flavor."
—*Encounters,* The Science Museum of Minnesota

"Even the most up-to-date Minnesota-ologist could learn a few things from this plain-talking, no-frills paperback."
—*St. Paul Pioneer Press*

Minnesota

OFF THE
BEATEN
PATH™

THIRD EDITION

JOHN G. SHEPARD

A Voyager Book

The Globe Pequot Press

Old Saybrook, Connecticut

The quotes and references to architectural historians on pages 47, 64, and 77 are from *A Guide to the Architecture of Minnesota,* by David Gebhard and Tom Martinson, University of Minnesota Press, 1977.

Illustrations by Carole Drong

Cover map copyright © DeLorme Mapping

Library of Congress Cataloging-in-Publication Data
Shepard, John G.
    Minnesota : off the beaten path / by John G. Shepard. — 3rd ed.
        p.   cm. — (Off the beaten path series)
    "A Voyager book."
    Includes index.
    ISBN 1-56440-498-6
    1. Minnesota—Guidebooks.   I. Title.   II. Series.
F604.3.S53   1995
917.7604'53—dc20   94-43644
                                                                          CIP

Manufactured in the United States of America
Third Edition/Third Printing

For Anna and Nat,
two intrepid travelers

MINNESOTA

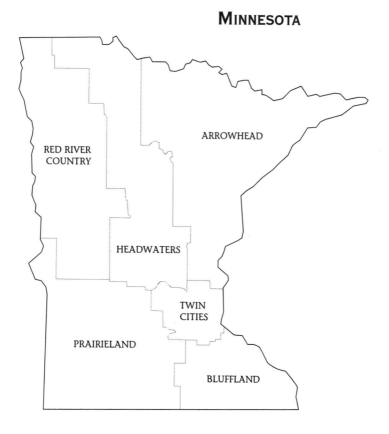

RED RIVER
COUNTRY

ARROWHEAD

HEADWATERS

TWIN
CITIES

PRAIRIELAND

BLUFFLAND

Contents

INTRODUCTION

Minnesota: Off the Beaten Path™ is an adventure through a landscape of sweeping contrasts and delightful surprises.

To the south and west is rolling prairie country. At one time or another, it has been range for bands of Plains Indians, massive herds of bison, legendary (if not mythical) Viking explorers, and generations of stoic, sodbusting Norwegian and German farmers. A day's drive to the northeast leads into the heart of Minnesota's densely forested and lake-strewn wilderness. Over the centuries these woodlands have hosted French fur traders, thousands of miners from all over Europe, and an equal number of larger-than-life lumberjacks, both whimsical and real. And in between, straddling the high banks of the Mississippi River, are Minneapolis and St. Paul. These two eminently cosmopolitan cities trace their present glory to an unlikely and at times most unloving marriage of Protestant millers, Irish Catholic railroad magnates, and German beer barons.

Stray even slightly from the beaten path in such an environment and there's no telling *where* you might wind up. It could be in a squat canvas tent observing the bizarre courtship rituals of the prairie chicken. Or it could be enjoying an incomparable Mississippi River sunset from the roof of a chartered houseboat. But no matter how unexpected the turn of events, if the people around you are refreshingly civil and sometimes use quaint expressions like "Uff-da" and "You betcha," know that you aren't really lost—you're just somewhere off the beaten path in Minnesota.

The more than 300 destination descriptions in this book were selected following extensive firsthand field research. The more intriguing among them make up the legends accompanying the regional maps. Taken together, all the destinations reflect the full breadth of attractions that Minnesota has to offer those travelers willing to venture down the road less traveled. There are sites of historical, geological, and archaeological interest; novel recreational opportunities; unusual restaurants, taverns, shops, and country inns; unique events and festivals; buildings of special architectural significance; compelling tours; fascinating museums and art galleries; and those occasional phenomena that refuse to be pigeonholed. As much as possible, these interest areas have been represented equally in each region of the state.

Consult the index if you are having trouble locating a specific destination in the text.

To guide you efficiently into blissful obscurity and then get you back home again, this guide is organized around Minnesota's most prominent geographical and historical divisions. Each area has its own distinctive character arising from nature's varied endowments and the accidents of human history.

The Twin Cities chapter includes Minneapolis and St. Paul as well as the outlying seven-county metropolitan area. The world-class cultural attractions of the Twin Cities are complemented by extensive park systems and the beautiful valleys of the Mississippi, St. Croix, and Minnesota rivers.

Bluffland is found in Minnesota's southeastern corner, where clear-flowing streams wind through deep hardwood valleys to join the Mississippi River. The area's rugged landscape, which was spared a scouring by the glaciers of the last ice age, is unique to the state. Along meandering byways through dozens of charming little towns you'll find rich history and gracious hospitality.

Prairieland is that sweep of gently rolling country southwest of Minneapolis and St. Paul. The lovely Minnesota River valley has nurtured a string of fascinating towns and historic sites relating to one of the country's most tragic wars between Indians and settlers. Remaining areas of virgin prairie, which in summer are ablaze with wildflowers, offer glimpses of the land as it appeared before the onslaught of the plow.

Red River Country embraces Minnesota's northwestern corner, all of which drains into the Red River of the North and eventually into Hudson Bay. Moorhead is the cultural center of this alluvial plain, which boasts some of the richest agricultural land on earth.

The Headwaters region encompasses north-central Minnesota, where the Mississippi River begins its epic journey to the sea. In its northern reaches this area is forested and still largely undeveloped. Then, as America's mightiest river curves southward in the shape of a huge question mark, the surrounding landscape is increasingly dotted by farms and the granite quarries of St. Cloud.

The Arrowhead—really more of a triangle in shape—extends north and east of the Twin Cities to form a sharp tip along the dramatic north shore of Lake Superior. Outdoor activities in and around the pristine Boundary Waters Canoe Area wilderness and Voyageurs National Park run from dogsledding to kayaking to walleye fishing. The area also abounds in interpretive sites related to fur trade, logging, shipping, and mining history. The cultural center of the Arrowhead is Duluth—Minnesota's exciting inland seaport.

Wherever appropriate, telephone numbers and addresses are listed in the text for you to obtain more information on particular sites. The Minnesota Office of Tourism is an outstanding source of assistance in the event that some of these listings become outdated (call toll-free from within Minnesota, 800–652–9747; from outside Minnesota, 800–328–1461; or from the Twin Cities, 296–5029). Official state highway maps are also available by calling these numbers.

Except where indicated otherwise, prices in the text are described in general terms according to the following rough guidelines. Meals in restaurants are deemed inexpensive or modest if under $10, moderately priced if $10 to $20, and expensive if above $20. Accommodations are listed as modest or inexpensive if under $40, moderately priced if $40 to $100, and expensive if above $100. Admission prices are termed token, modest, or inexpensive if under $5; moderately priced if $5 to $20; and expensive if above $20. The prices and rates listed in this guidebook were accurate at press time, but I recommend that you call establishments before traveling in order to get the most up-to-date information.

TWIN CITIES

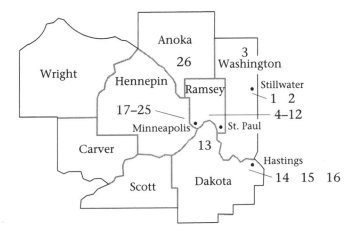

1. Minnesota Zephyr
2. Washington County
   Historical Society
3. Crabtree's Kitchen
4. Alexander Ramsey House
5. Forepaugh's restaurant
6. No Wake Cafe
7. St. Paul Gangster Tours
8. Children's Museum
9. Russian Piroshki and Teahouse
10. Old Muskego Church
11. Goldstein Gallery
12. Gibbs Farm Museum
13. Sibley House
14. Thorwood B&B

15. LeDuc-Simmons Mansion
16. Alexis Bailly Vineyard
17. Upper St. Anthony Lock
    and Dam
18. Historic Fort Snelling
19. Minnehaha Falls
20. Foshay Tower
21. American Swedish Institute
22. Bakken Library and Museum
23. Pavek Museum of
    Broadcasting
24. Firefighters Museum
25. Planes of Fame War Birds
    Air Museum
26. Bunker Hills Wave Pool

TWIN CITIES

WASHINGTON COUNTY

It is claimed that Minnesota was born at the charming Washington County seat of Stillwater, where in 1848 a cadre of visionary pioneer settlers gathered to proclaim Minnesota's territorial status. Out of the wilderness they dispatched a fur trader named Henry Hastings Sibley to convince the U.S. Congress of their legitimacy. The following year Sibley won official recognition on behalf of his group and Minnesota was on the map.

Nearly a century and a half later, **Stillwater** persists as a living museum of nineteenth-century history and architecture that is blessed with one of the loveliest settings imaginable. Nestled in a pocket formed in the bluffs of the St. Croix River on the outside of a bend, the town centers on a commercial district of antiques shops, boutiques, and restaurants in historic buildings that line an attractive riverside park. The waterfront is alive with boat traffic spring through autumn, when across the river Wisconsin's undeveloped wooded shoreline explodes in fall color. Any one of the steep streets leading uphill from the center of town passes well-preserved residences, churches, and buildings representing numerous Victorian architectural styles (call the Chamber of Commerce at 612–439–7700 for information on **walking and auto tours** of Stillwater's historic buildings).

The ◆**Minnesota Zephyr,** a late-1940s dining train, cruises railroad tracks that parallel the beautiful St. Croix River for a distance before climbing atop the bluff to travel through a rolling pastoral landscape. While taking in the view, passengers can enjoy fillet of flounder, game hen, or prime rib as the centerpiece of an expensive five-course meal. The Zephyr operates year-round (thanks to a new winterized depot), weekend evenings. Weekday evenings are added to the schedule when weekends fill up. Call (612) 430–3000 well in advance to make reservations.

For those wishing to learn more about Stillwater's history, a visit is in order to the former warden's residence of the territorial prison, which now serves as the ◆**Washington County Historical Society.** You'll find this 1850s-era stone structure at 602 North Main Street in a little canyon known as Battle Hollow;

legend has it that two warring Dakota and Ojibway chiefs fought a duel to the death at this spot. Guides at the museum will lead you through a variety of exhibits concerning Stillwater's early prominence as a lumber town, life in the penitentiary, and other aspects of county history. A small fee is charged for admission to the museum, which is open Tuesdays, Thursdays, Saturdays, and Sundays, May through October or by special arrangement. Call (612) 439–5956 for more information.

As Minnesota 95 runs north out of Stillwater, it climbs a deep, wooded ravine and follows the edge of the St. Croix valley to the quiet little village of Marine on St. Croix. Like most towns along the river, Marine enjoyed early prosperity from the logging boom of the last half of the nineteenth century, resulting in the construction of a number of stately historic homes. Among them is one outstanding example of the Greek Revival style, a bed-and-breakfast establishment named after its builder, Asa Parker, a founder of one of Marine's lumber mills. The warmth of the fireplace, hospitality, and delicious full breakfasts prepared by Marjorie Bush, owner of the **Asa Parker House**, provide a soothing retreat at day's end. Several rooms have beautiful views of the valley, and all offer antique decorations, tasteful wall coverings, private baths, and the small touches—fresh flowers, potpourri—that make for a memorable stay. Prices are moderate to expensive. For more information and reservations, call (612) 433–5248.

If you don't feel like making the drive from Marine on St. Croix back to Stillwater for lunch and dinner, a couple of local eateries may well suit your tastes. Facing the Marine town square on Main Street is the hole-in-the-wall **Voyageur Cafe**, which serves inexpensive sandwiches on homemade bread, soups, and other tasty items made of fresh ingredients. A couple of miles north of Marine, in the tiny hamlet of Copas, is ◆**Crabtree's Kitchen,** which offers traditional American fare in a dining room filled with early American antiques. From late November until mid-December each year, Crabtree's serves traditional Scandinavian *lutefisk* (cod cured in lye) with Swedish meatballs and sausage, and for those who can't wait until winter, this menu is sometimes made available for a few days in late August. Horse-drawn sleigh rides on weekends from late November through February round out the scene at Crabtree's. For more information call (612) 433–2455.

3

RAMSEY COUNTY

St. Paul had its start as a ragged frontier settlement clustered about a tavern on the banks of the Mississippi. The proprietor of this saloon was a notoriously uncouth and licentious sixty-year-old ex-voyageur known as Pig's Eye Parrant. After one of his customers successfully used "Pig's Eye" as a return mailing address on a letter, this flattering name fell into use in reference to the settlement as a whole. Then, in 1840, the Catholic Church sent a missionary to serve the needs of the area's settlers and the soldiers at nearby Fort Snelling. Father Lucian Galtier built a log chapel in honor of St. Paul near Parrant's saloon and eventually succeeded in promoting the use of this Christian name instead of the decidedly heathen one already in service.

From these humble beginnings St. Paul's location at the head of navigation on the Mississippi River resulted in decades of explosive growth, as huge numbers of settlers streamed upriver from St. Louis to stake their claims on the northern frontier. Territorial status was achieved a mere nine years after Galtier's arrival, and Minnesota found itself under the leadership of a young Pennsylvanian named Alexander Ramsey, who served as Minnesota's first territorial governor and second state governor. Today the ◆ **Alexander Ramsey House,** at 265 South Exchange Street, provides some fascinating glimpses into this remarkable era of St. Paul's and Minnesota's infancy.

Your tour of the fifteen-room, French Second Empire–style limestone mansion begins in the carriage house/gift shop with a video program on the governor's career. Then a costumed guide leads you into the outer parlor, where, had you been a female acquaintance of Mrs. (Anna) Ramsey's and of proper standing, you might have paid a highly ritualized "call." Staying no more than fifteen to twenty minutes and being careful to discuss only the appropriate topics (politics and religion were taboo), you would then have been free to proceed to your next stop confident that Minnesota's First Lady was obliged to return the favor of your visit. The governor, however, dispensed with this formality by ushering his male guests via a side door to his second-floor office, where you can bet that discussions of politics and other contentious subjects were the rule.

Alexander Ramsey House

The exquisitely preserved house, which remained within the family until it was willed to the Minnesota Historical Society in the 1960s, retains almost all of its original furnishings and many of the innovations (such as running hot water upstairs) that made it a noteworthy structure in its time. Tours last an hour and are given for a small fee daily except for Sundays and Mondays, April through December. A special Victorian Christmas celebration is held each year from Thanksgiving to New Years. For more information call (612) 296–0100.

To preserve the Victorian spell cast by the atmosphere of the Ramsey House, you need do no more than cross the street to 276 South Exchange Street, where the elegant ◆**Forepaugh's restaurant** serves fine French cuisine in the former home of one of the Ramsey's acquaintances. The grand, two-story, Italianate structure has been lavishly decorated in the spirit of the late 1800s, when it was built for Joseph Forepaugh, owner of the largest wholesale dry-goods dealership in the Northwest. Prices are moderate to expensive. For reservations call (612) 224–5606.

On the other hand, following your tour of the Ramsey House you may have had your fill of Victorian life. If so, you can always cross the Wabasha Street bridge and head down to the Mississippi riverbank on Harriet Island for a floating meal at the ◆**No Wake Cafe.** This intimate houseboat-restaurant affords a great view of downtown St. Paul and the boats and cumbersome barges that cruise the river. The home-cooked meals are a savory bargain, too. The No Wake serves breakfast and lunch Tuesday through Thursday, a special fish dinner on Wednesdays, and breakfast, lunch, and dinner, Friday through Sunday. It is closed in the winter.

In the very early 1900s, St. Paul Police Chief John O'Connor set up a system that provided a safe haven for criminals of all types, provided they obeyed the laws while in the city. Though O'Connor stepped down from his post in 1920, his system remained in place. The result was that, from the late 20s to mid-30s, during the heyday of Prohibition and the Depression, St. Paul served as "home safe home" to some of the most notorious gangsters of the twentieth century.

◆ **St. Paul Gangster Tours** provide an outstanding way to learn about this era. A couple of costumed guides host the two-hour tour to the city's most famous gangster hangouts and hideaways. You'll see the apartment complex where John Dillinger shot it out with St. Paul's finest and the sites of the Hamm and Bremer kidnappings. You'll also visit the post office where the Barker Gang pulled off the Swift Payroll Robbery. All the while your guides will regale you with stories about the likes of "Baby Face" Nelson, "Machine Gun" Kelly, and Alvin "Creepy" Karpis.

The moderately priced Gangster Tours are held one Saturday each month and depart from the St. Paul Hotel. Private tours, which can include lunch and dinner packages, can be arranged. For reservations and information call (612) 292–1220 or write St. Paul Gangster Tours, 827 Portland Avenue, St. Paul 55104.

The Memorial Concourse of the **St. Paul City Hall and Ramsey County Courthouse** has been well preserved as an Art Deco masterpiece and as one of the capital city's most noted architectural landmarks. Entering the narrow, three-story room feels a little like entering a hallowed chamber in the city of Oz. Very dark blue Belgian marble on the walls creates a mysteriously somber atmosphere. A mirrored ceiling reflects your every move and lends even greater apparent stature to the *Vision of Peace* statue that stands at the far end of the room. Made of sixty tons of luminous white onyx by Swedish sculptor Carl Milles, the 36-foot statue depicts five Native Americans in a spiritual ceremony, with a common godlike vision—of Peace—rising among them. The St. Paul City Hall and Ramsey County Courthouse, 15 West Kellogg Avenue in downtown St. Paul, is open to the public, free of charge.

Learning through hands-on exploration of some of the most unlikely objects is the key to fun at the ◆ **Children's Museum,** located near Bandana Square shopping mall in St. Paul. Don't be fooled by the name of this place, either—many adults, as well as kids, will enjoy filming one another in a television studio with real video cameras or operating a large electromagnetic crane. There is also an elaborate "underground" maze system, a mock radio station, a toddler playroom, and, befitting the building's former incarnation as a blacksmith's shop within the historic Burlington Northern railroad yards, a scaled-down steam engine, among many other artifacts of this and former ages.

The Children's Museum regularly holds special events involving its own theatrical troupe and in cooperation with other arts and educational programs in the Twin Cities. There is also a gift shop full of creative surprises. The museum is open Tuesday through Saturday year-round for a modest admission fee. It is located at 1217 Bandana Boulevard North, near Lexington Boulevard and behind the Bandana Square shopping center. For information on special events, call (612) 644–3818.

Traffic on University Avenue—one of the first roadways to connect Minneapolis and St. Paul—has always run thick and fast, which is a pity, because many people zip by the ◆ **Russian Piroshki and Teahouse** never knowing what they've missed. When Nikolai Alenov opened this modest take-out place in 1978, it was one of the first Russian fast-food restaurants in the country. Since then, his mother's recipe for piroshki, or Russian hamburgers—heavenly dumplings filled with ground beef, rice, and spices that are either deep-fried or baked—has attracted a loyal clientele of office workers and neighbors. Nikolai also serves borscht, stuffed cabbage rolls, and, of course, Russian tea, all at very inexpensive prices. A couple of tables have recently been added if you'd prefer to eat in. To find this humble establishment, which is open Tuesday through Friday for lunch and early dinners, keep your eyes peeled for the sign at 1758 University on the south side of the street, just east of Fairview.

Another slice of regional history has been well preserved on the grounds of the Luther Seminary in the quiet neighborhood of St. Anthony Park. Here, tucked behind several classroom and administration buildings on top of a hill, is an attractive log building, the ◈**Old Muskego Church,** which stands as a living monument to the first organized Norwegian Lutheran congregation in the New World.

As the door to the lovely old church swings open, there is an aroma of aged red oak and walnut that is as strong as frankincense. One's attention is drawn immediately to the front of the chancel, where, in oriental-like simplicity and grace, a solid walnut, five-sided altar sits below a turret-shaped pulpit, whose prominence in the building reflects the importance of the spoken Word in the worship of the day. The straight-backed pews, the rough-hewn benches on the balcony, and the grim portraits of some of the early pastors convey something of the life these settlers led. Having chosen a swamp-infested site for their community near Milwaukee, Wisconsin, the settlers experienced a staggering incidence of death by cholera during the first few years (1843 to 1847). But the settlement finally prospered, producing the country's first two Norwegian newspapers, the first elected officials of Norwegian descent, and even a Civil War hero. The church was moved to its present site in 1904 and was added to the National Register of Historic Places in 1974. The building is open for self-guided tours daily, requiring only that you check in at the Seminary Information Desk in the Olson Campus Center building on the southeast corner of Hendon Avenue and Fulham Street.

The St. Paul campus of the University of Minnesota was developed originally as a "farm school," and the study of agricultural science is still a primary activity there. But within the School of Home Economics in the attractive McNeal Hall (1985 Buford Avenue) is an unusual exhibit gallery dedicated to common objects of human design—clothing, textiles, household items, and decorative arts. Exhibits at the small ◈**Goldstein Gallery** change every two to three months and cover a broad range of themes, from underwear making to the history of inventions by women. The gallery is open daily, free of charge; for information on current exhibits, call (612) 624–7434.

As the expanding populations of the Twin Cities pushed the city limits ever closer to each other around the turn of the century, the Heman Gibbs family on the northern perimeter of this "interurban zone" adapted their farming practices to the growing urban market. By planting a greater variety of fruits and vegetables and by rushing their fresh produce to the farmer's market each day, they joined ranks with a little-known agricultural tradition called the urban-fringe farm. Their farmhouse, with its original furnishings, and the outbuildings used by the Gibbs family have been preserved as the ◈ **Gibbs Farm Museum,** located at Larpenteur and Cleveland avenues in Falcon Heights, where the clock has been set back to 1901.

Guided tours of the farm begin with a short slide show and then lead through a one-room schoolhouse, two barns, and the house, where something's frequently cooking on the woodstove in the summer kitchen. On Sundays staff and volunteers in period dress provide demonstrations of such tasks as candle dipping, butter churning, doll making, and quilting, to name only a few. The educational practices of the time are explained by a teacher holding forth at the blackboard. And during special festivals it's not unheard of for staff and volunteers to kick up their heels and dance or to compete in such contests as seeing who can produce the most attractive shawl starting with a mass of uncarded wool. The museum is open for a small fee Tuesday through Sunday, planting time through harvest. Call (612) 646–8629 for more information.

"From Urban Places to Country Spaces" is the motto of the recently completed **Gateway Trail,** an old "rail trail" that connects St. Paul to Stillwater, and it couldn't be more accurate. The trail runs for 17.1 miles from Arlington Avenue in St. Paul to Pine Point Park, 5 miles north of Stillwater. For its first few miles, the trail provides a nice alternative to busy highways as it passes through the communities of East St. Paul, Maplewood, and North St. Paul.

Then, after passing beneath Interstate 694, the Gateway Trail becomes decidedly pastoral as it meanders past many ponds, barns, and marshes in a gently rolling landscape. The primary trail is paved, providing an ideal surface for bicycles and roller blades. An adjacent gravel trail runs beside it, which can be used by horses and mountain bikes. Steep grades are few and access points many, making the Gateway Trail quite user-friendly. For maps and more information, contact the Minnesota DNR Information Center, 500 Lafayette Road, St. Paul 55155 or call (800) 766–6000.

If you are one of the many poor souls allergic to domed stadiums and plastic grass, a visit to a **St. Paul Saints** baseball game could be just what the doctor ordered. The Saints, who play forty home games a year at Municipal Stadium (north of Snelling on Energy Park Drive), are members of the Northern League, a six-team independent league, whose teams aren't affiliated with Major League parent clubs. The play is not quite of Major League caliber, but the games are fast paced, and the between-innings entertainment is at least half the fun. Tickets are inexpensively to moderately priced. For reservations or information call 644–6659.

DAKOTA COUNTY

The geographical hub around which much of Minnesota's history has revolved is the confluence of the Minnesota and Mississippi rivers. In 1805, two years after the Louisiana Purchase gave the United States access to the Mississippi watershed, the territory surrounding this strategic junction of Minnesota's two largest rivers was obtained through treaty from the Dakota Indians for sixty gallons of whiskey and $2,000 worth of trade goods. The land wasn't occupied by its new owners, however, until fourteen years later, when 200 soldiers spent a miserable winter (forty of them died of scurvy) camped near the site of what was to become Fort Snelling, Minnesota's first military outpost and the Northwest's most remote fort for thirty years. (See Hennepin County, page 13.)

Eventually the Twin Cities sprang up in proximity to this spot—St. Paul a few miles downstream, at the head of navigation on the Mississippi, and Minneapolis at a roughly equal distance upstream on the same river, where the once-magnificent St. Anthony Falls provided waterpower for early industry. But well before either city was established, Minnesota's first permanent white settlement took root in Fort Snelling's protective shadow on the southern banks of the Minnesota-Mississippi confluence.

Mendota (from the Dakota Indian word for "where the waters mingle"), as the town is called now, grew around a fur trade post run by Henry Hastings Sibley of the American Fur Company. A visit to the ❖ **Sibley House,** a historic site operated by the Daughters of the American Revolution, reveals much about this pioneer statesman and the era in which he lived.

A year after his arrival in 1834, Sibley and a group of fellow traders and local Indians built the handsome limestone dwelling as a home and business center. As you enter its large entry, a glass wall panel reveals an innovative building process: The interior walls combined river mud, sand, and clay with a latticework of grass and woven willow branches. But despite the primitive materials used in its construction, the Sibley House was an oasis of civility on the frontier. Tasteful period furnishings in every room suggest how lucrative the fur trade was, while providing insight into the life-style of the Victorian society to which the Sibleys aspired. A "fainting couch" placed at the top of the stairs was available for tightly corseted ladies who may have arrived upstairs short of breath. In Mrs. Sibley's bedroom a bootjack features a decorative panel positioned so as to have prevented anyone present from glimpsing her emerging ankle.

The Sibley House is adjacent to the Faribault House, built by the fur trader Jean Baptiste Faribault and operated now as a museum, with exhibits on the fur trade and the Dakota and Ojibway Indian cultures.

Both houses are open Tuesday through Sunday for a small fee from May through October; they are also open weekends in October when they are decorated for Christmas. Living-history demonstrations are scheduled occasionally. Both are located along Minnesota 13 on the west end of the town of Mendota. For more information call (612) 452–1596.

Hastings—located about 20 miles downstream of Mendota at the junction of the Mississippi, St. Croix, and Vermillion rivers—is another community that owes its early existence to the flowing waters at its doorstep. This Dakota County seat of 13,000 retains much charm from its heyday in the second half of the nineteenth century, when water-powered grain mills made the city one of the greatest wheat markets of the Northwest. A drive down the old main street, Second Avenue, reveals many original storefronts still intact.

Another way to enjoy Hastings's rich architectural heritage is to take a self-guided **front-porch tour** of the historic district, following directions in a brochure available from the Chamber of Commerce at 427 Vermillion Street. In fact the town has become so enthralled by its eclectic porches that on a weekend in early May an annual **Front Porch Festival** is held to rekindle memories of the time when front porches were a focal point of neighborhood social life in America. The festival features house and porch tours, clinics on porch and home reconstruction, horse-and-buggy rides, and historic games (call 612–437–6775 for more information).

Two of Hastings's gracious older homes open their doors to visitors as exceptional bed-and-breakfasts operated by Pam and Dick Thorsen. The grand ✦ **Thorwood B&B,** the center of the operation, is an 1880 French Second Empire house with a steeple reaching skyward above the roof line. The award-winning Queen Anne–style Rosewood dates from the same year. The Thorsens have tastefully renovated both houses in keeping with their original designs while retaining some features that recall their one-time incarnations as small hospitals.

At Thorwood evidence of a vertical shaft persists from the hospital's primitive hand-powered elevator. This "convenience" was unsuitable for use by pregnant women, who were restricted from unduly exerting themselves on the hand-operated controls. Instead they had to use the stairs. Patients on stretchers were unable to fit into the small enclosure without standing up. The Lullaby room is popular with some locals who slept there when it served as the hospital nursery.

All of the fifteen rooms at the two B&Bs have private baths, some equipped with double whirlpools, and eleven of them have wood-burning fireplaces. Innovative room service is offered at both establishments, including delicious multicourse "hatbox" suppers served in real hatboxes, and extravagant seasonal theme suppers, such as the "Dickens of a Dinner," delivered replete with a hard-cover volume of Dickens's prose. Of course full breakfasts are provided as well. Rates for lodging and breakfast are moderate to expensive; packages including dinner are expensive. For more information or reservations, call (612) 437–3297 or (800) 657–4630.

What else to do in Hastings? The ✦ **LeDuc-Simmons Mansion,** one of the few remaining nineteenth-century Hudson River

Gothic Revival dwellings in the country, is worth a stroll by its address at 1629 Vermillion Street. Farther south on Vermillion Street you will cross the Vermillion River, where just to the east is the beginning of a lovely park around a dramatic waterfall. The ruins of the **Ramsey Mill** can be explored downstream where the river rounds a bend.

Continuing out of town south on Highway 61, in 1 mile you'll see signs for Minnesota's only full-fledged vineyard. The approach to the production facilities of ◆**Alexis Bailly Vineyard** is through a field of more than 6,000 hybrid grape vines that are especially well suited to Minnesota's harsh winter climate. The wine these grapes produce has received national recognition for its excellence. Visitors are welcome to taste-test the Bailly wines and to observe the fermenting process. The vineyard is open free of charge from June through October, Friday through Sunday afternoons. For more information call (612) 437–1413.

HENNEPIN COUNTY

By the late nineteenth century, Minneapolis's flour mills had earned the city a reputation as the flour capital of the world, a reputation dependent on the tremendous waterpower generated by the Falls of St. Anthony. By far the largest drop in the Mississippi's 2,348-mile run to the sea, the falls, with their unstable limestone base, have precipitated some extensive engineering projects over the years. Today they are covered with concrete, and two locks—one 50 and the other 25 feet deep—provide passage for barges, pleasure boats, and an occasional canoe. An observation deck at the ◆**Upper St. Anthony Lock and Dam,** with displays and brochures explaining the operation of the lock and the history of the falls area, is open daily from April through November (a parking area is located near the corner of Portland and Washington avenues). For information call 333–5336.

Built between 1819 and 1825 as Minnesota's first permanent structure, ◆**Historic Fort Snelling** still dominates the confluence of the Mississippi and Minnesota rivers from a prominent bluff several miles downstream of St. Anthony Falls. The fort has been restored to its original appearance and is superbly managed by the Minnesota Historical Society as a popular interpretive center and living-history site. Daily, from May through October, a contingent of soldiers in heavy wool uniforms reenact with humor and robust spirit the highly regimented and often-tedious life led by the early occupants of this military outpost, which, for all its apparent might, has never seen a moment of fighting. Look for the fort at the junction of Highways 5 and 55 (there are signs on both highways, but don't confuse the historic fort with Fort Snelling State Park, also close by). A small fee is charged for admission to the fort but not to the adjacent interpretive center, where an excellent exhibit space, film-viewing area, and gift shop are open whenever the fort is and on weekdays the rest of the year. Call (612) 726–1171 for more information.

Though he never traveled to the northwestern wilderness, Henry Wadsworth Longfellow helped create in the nation's imagination a highly romantic impression of the Minnesota frontier through his epic 1855 poem, *The Song of Hiawatha.* In particular the story of Hiawatha's courtship of Minnehaha endowed two landmarks with mythical significance: the "shining Big-Sea-Water" of "Gitche Gumee" (Lake Superior) and a waterfall along a small Minneapolis creek from which the lovely maiden received her identity. "From the waterfall he named her, / Minnehaha, Laughing Water" wrote Longfellow, and ◆ **Minnehaha Falls** hasn't been the same since. Visitors to the burgeoning metropolis during Longfellow's time flocked to see Minnehaha's laughing waters, which are just as inspiring today, as you can discover for yourself by heading a couple of blocks east on Minnehaha Parkway from the intersection of (what else?) Hiawatha Avenue.

Given what you can see of the Minneapolis skyline from afar, you might easily suspect that the entire city has been built within the past ten or fifteen years. While it's true that most buildings with enough stature to be seen from any distance away are new and reflect an innovative variety of current architectural tastes, there is still one remnant of earlier times that now reaches only chest height of its taller neighbors. This is the ◆ **Foshay Tower,** an obelisk design inspired by the Washington Monument and built as an ostentatious monument to prosperity on the verge of the stockmarket crash of 1929 by one of the city's more interesting public figures.

Wilber Foshay, a newly rich utility-company owner, spent almost $4 million in the construction of this first skyscraper west of Chicago and then took the trouble to seek two patents on its design so that it would never be duplicated elsewhere. He planned to install himself in a lavish penthouse suite that complemented the building's Art Deco styling with a vaulted entry, rich woodwork, and gold-plated faucets.

For the grand opening of his tower, Foshay invited President Hoover (the war secretary came in his stead), along with every state governor in the country. He also commissioned John Philip Sousa to write a march in honor of the occasion, a work the celebrated composer directed in person.

Two months later Foshay's entire dream crumbled around him in the wake of Black Thursday's stockmarket plunge. Not only was he unable to pay the bills for the lavish party he had thrown; he was also indicted for mail fraud by the federal government. Foshay spent some time in Leavenworth Prison before being pardoned by President Roosevelt in 1935. He died in a Twin Cities nursing home in 1957, leaving his monument behind for us to visit today. Self-guided tours of the observation deck, which has outstanding views of the cityscape and surrounding countryside, and a small museum devoted to the building's history are available during business hours and on Saturdays for a small fee. You'll find the Foshay Tower by tracing its unmistakable shape to its foundation at 821 Marquette Avenue. Call 341–2522 for more information.

Another less-celebrated monument to posterity is found in Minneapolis's ✦**American Swedish Institute** (2600 Park Avenue), which helped to inspire a movement to preserve Swedish culture that was initiated by the building's first owner, Swan J. Turnblad. This Swedish-born businessman built a thirty-three-room Romanesque château–style castle for himself that was financed by his success as a publisher of America's largest Swedish newspaper, the *Svenska Amerikanska Posten*. He lived in his turn-of-the-century mansion only a relatively short time, donating the building and his collection of Swedish art and historic artifacts to the institute in 1929.

It is an amazing building. The elaborate turrets and carvings of the limestone exterior only half prepare you for the incredible woodwork and rich ornamentation found inside. Eighteen craftspersons worked for two years to complete the intricately carved statues, panels, and banisters—all made of exotic woods—that you continue to discover throughout your tour. There are eleven unique *kakelugnar* Swedish stoves made of porcelain tile.

15

And at the first-floor stair landing is a grand stained-glass window based on a historic painting that depicts, of all things, the ransom of a Swedish community by a Danish king.

Rooms on three floors of the institute are dedicated to exhibits on contemporary and historic Swedish artists and to the immigration experience. Perhaps the most unusual item on display is a pre-Viking glass beaker dating from the fifth century A.D. and believed to be among the earliest glass objects in the world. The institute also frequently shows films and has public programs related to Swedish culture. The building is open for tours Tuesday through Sunday, year-round, for a small fee. For more information call (612) 871–4907.

On an obscure side street near the western shore of Lake Calhoun, one of Minneapolis's lovely urban lakes, is a singularly fascinating museum and library dedicated to the role electricity has played in our science and culture. Upon entering the 1920s English Tudor–style mansion that houses the ❖**Bakken Library and Museum,** you are confronted immediately with several aquariums of electricity-producing fish. The thoroughly informed guide who meets you here explains that as early as the first century A.D., these creatures were employed by the Romans in the treatment of arthritis. The afflicted patient was directed to go to the ocean shore and stand with one foot in the water and the other on top of one of these slithering fish, whose sensible response was to blast the offending foot with as much juice as it could muster.

The Bakken tour moves quickly from ancient times to displays of eighteenth-century devices and procedural drawings that illustrate the first widespread use of electricity for public entertainment and in medicine. Electric "showers," in which a simple static generator produced a mild current, or "fluid," that was allowed to flow through the body, were thought to have an invigorating influence on the subject's health. More powerful localized applications via the "method of sparks" or, stronger still, the often painful "electric commotions" were used to cure anything from "hysteria" and other complaints thought to be peculiar to women to jolting patients from states of "suspended animation" resulting from drowning or heart failure.

In another room a series of nineteenth-century photographs reveals the results of an experiment in which the electrical stimulation of specific facial muscles was shown to produce in the same subject strained expressions covering the full spectrum of human emotion. A number of early X-ray machines are displayed, as is a picture of Alexander Graham Bell using an early electric metal detector to find a bullet in the body of President Garfield. If you feel the need, you can even get a charge yourself and watch your hair stand on end by placing a hand on an eighteenth-century Ramsden generator.

The Bakken museum and 12,000-volume reference library were established in 1976 by Earl Bakken, the inventor of the first wearable cardiac pacemaker. Tours are given for a modest fee, on Saturdays and by advance reservation Monday through Friday. For more information call (612) 927–6508.

The invention of the telegraph by Samuel Morse in 1835 portended great things for human communication. With the telegraph, for the first time in the history of the planet people could send messages halfway across the country in a matter of seconds. The only problem was that if the wires that carried these signals became damaged—as they frequently did in wild expanses of the largely unsettled North American continent—no message could be sent. So in 1895, after a series of experiments, Thomas Edison applied for a patent for his "Wireless Telegraph." With this device messages could be sent through the air via radio waves, and thus the age of radio was born.

From these forgotten beginnings the ◆ **Pavek Museum of Broadcasting** in St. Louis Park traces the growth of radio and broadcasting in a most delightful manner. Founded by radio collector and enthusiast Joseph Pavek in 1988, the museum houses an impressive collection of radios, phonographs, tape recorders, and other equipment. Bing Crosby sounds remarkably good crooning on a recording made on one of the very first tape recorders. The museum also has a working ham-radio center and a 1960s-vintage recording studio, often used by school children on field trips to write and produce their own radio program.

The whole place takes you back to a simpler time, when families used to gather in living rooms—Mom and Dad in their favorite chairs, the kids lying on the floor with their heads propped on their hands—and listen to the radio. Nowhere is this innocence better illustrated than in the Minnesota Room's collection of paraphernalia from our state's radio past. Hidden in one of the display cases is a membership card to the Cowboy Bill

17

Club (Cowboy Bill hosted a children's radio program in the 1930s and 1940s). Printed on the card are Cowboy Bill's Rules for Success:

1. Obey your parents.
2. Be cheerful.
3. Keep clean.
4. Save your money.

Ah, the good old days.

The Pavek Museum of Broadcasting, 3515 Raleigh Avenue, St. Louis Park 55416, is open Tuesdays through Saturdays, year-round. Admission is inexpensive. Call (612) 926–8198 for group reservations.

Are you someone who was convinced at least once in your life that being a firefighter is life's highest calling? If so, you might enjoy a visit to the ❖ **Firefighters Museum,** in northeast Minneapolis near the northwest corner of Broadway and Central, where you can indulge in the fantasy once again. From a 1796-vintage hand-drawn water pump to the 1940s engine that roars in and out of the building, siren wailing, loaded with kids for a ride through the neighborhood, there are dozens of engines and plenty of firefighting memorabilia to spark your childhood recollections or generate some new ones. Modern trucks from the 1940s, 1950s, and 1960s dominate one part of the museum, whereas a second area is dedicated to horse- and hand-drawn pumps. There are big-billed firefighters' hard hats and rubberized coats to try on for photographs (bring your own camera), pictures of historic Twin Cities fires in progress, and models of various firehouses. The museum is open on Saturdays and charges a small fee. To find it, take Broadway to Jackson and go north 1 block to Twelfth, east 1 block to Van Buren, and then south for 1 block. If you get lost, listen for sirens or call (612) 623–3817.

If you escaped childhood without ever having dreamed of being a firefighter, then perhaps the ❖ **Planes of Fame War Birds Air Museum** would be to your liking. Occupying three hangars at Flying Cloud Airport in Eden Prairie, the air museum's high-quality exhibits and film-viewing area complement a collection of more than twenty-four World War II–vintage fighters, including a B-17 Flying Fortress bomber, all restored and maintained in flight-ready condition. Exhibits feature model planes, uniforms, and rifles from the war. A partially dismantled engine from a B-17 Flying Fortress reveals the engine's inner workings. Among the action-packed aerial-combat and training films is one starring a spunky Ronald Reagan, describing how to distinguish a Japanese Zero fighter from an American plane when the sun's in your eyes. For a hefty fee you can even go up for a ride in an open-cockpit Stearman Trainer. There is a modest admission charge at the museum, which is open afternoons daily during summer and is located at 14771 Pioneer Trail (County Road 1). Call (612) 941–2633 for more information.

There's no better way to soothe your shattered nerves after a ride in the Stearman Trainer (or any other high-tech stress inducer) than to stroll at a leisurely pace through the **Normandale Japanese Gardens** at Normandale Community College in Bloomington. Created by Tokyo designer Takao Watanabe, the garden's large waterfall and creek, three arch bridges, lagoon, and shrine exude serenity. A self-guided tour booklet is available for a small fee, and guided tours can be arranged for groups of ten or more. To find the garden, look for signs at the entrance to the college at 9700 France Avenue South or call (612) 832–6303. The garden is always open, though the waterfall is turned off October through May. Sunsets are lovely.

ANOKA COUNTY

Whatever Minnesota lacks in seascapes it makes up for in its oceanic enthusiasm for the state's one and only wave pool. Never mind that each twenty-minute set of computer-generated, air-powered waves lapses into a hiatus of unnatural calm while lifeguards conduct a safety check. A wave is still a wave, and a beach a beach (albeit a cement one), and that makes the ◆ **Bunker Hills Wave Pool** one of the Twin Cities' hot spots for summer frolic and fun.

On hot, sunny days, when every wave may be filled almost to capacity and all available inner tubes rented (you can't bring your own, and surfboards aren't allowed), you may want to plan your visit for late morning or late afternoon, when the crowds diminish. Then you might even be able to actually catch a wave and ride it somewhere other than directly into someone's lap.

When you've absorbed enough kinetic energy from the pulsing waves (which can be generated in four styles up to 4 feet high), you can enjoy those other quintessential beach pursuits: sun and snooze. Sand-court volleyball, concessions (you can't bring your own food or drinks), camping, horseback riding, and hiking and biking trails are also found in the park.

You can find Bunker Hills Regional Park north of Coon Rapids on Minnesota 242 at Foley Boulevard. The wave pool is open daily from 10:00 A.M. to 7:00 P.M. for a small fee from Memorial Day weekend through Labor Day. For more information call (612) 755–3672.

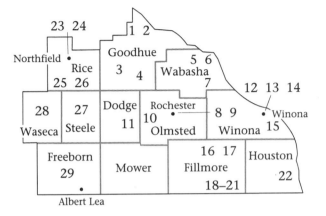

1. St. James Hotel
2. Redwing Stoneware Co.
3. Ordovician fossils
4. Covered bridge
5. Arrowhead Bluffs Exhibits
6. Anderson House
7. L.A.R.K. Toys
8. Mayo Clinic
9. Mayowood
10. Oxbow Park
11. Hubbell House
12. Polish Museum
13. Conway Universal Studios
14. Bunnell House
15. Pickwick Mill
16. Root River State Trail
17. Southeastern Minnesota Forest Resource Center
18. Niagara Cave
19. Mystery Cave
20. Thomas Meighen's Farm Village
21. Steam Engine Museum
22. Schech's Mill
23. Northfield Historical Society
24. Archer House
25. Faribo Mill
26. Cathedral of our Merciful Savior
27. Norwest Bank
28. Farmamerica
29. Myre–Big Island State Park

BLUFFLAND

GOODHUE COUNTY

When you enter the picturesque Mississippi River town of Red Wing from any direction, it's hard not to notice **Barn Bluff**, an oblong mountain that rises abruptly 300 feet above the heart of the business district like the back of some great subterranean elephant. Thousands of years ago this protrusion of ancient sandstone was an island surrounded by a much larger and glacial Mississippi River. Today Barn Bluff offers hikers the same grand views of the city and river environment as it did when Henry David Thoreau climbed to its peak in 1861.

Several hiking trails begin at the base of the mountain near the east end of Fifth Street. One trail winds through an old sandstone quarry that overlooks the river, while another passes near the remains of a large limestone kiln that was used in the late nineteenth century. A third trail ascends to the crest of the mountain and follows its ridge from one end to the other, offering great vistas of the town on one side and the wooded channels of the Mississippi on the other. Still another trail follows the southern side of Barn Bluff and allows hikers to peer into backyards all over town.

About the time of Thoreau's visit, Red Wing was well on its way to becoming the world's largest primary wheat market. This economic activity drew businessmen from all over the country, prompting local boosters in 1875 to build a monument to the town's prosperity in the form of a first-class hotel and restaurant. Thanks to an extensive and faithful restoration effort in 1979, the ✦**St. James Hotel** today offers the same luxurious accommodations and excellent dining that it did more than a hundred years ago, when the *Minneapolis Mail* proclaimed the hotel was "second to none in the state, in arrangement, elegance of furniture and general appointment."

Graciously decorated and spacious guest rooms—many offering fine views of the river—are furnished with Victorian-era antiques and antique reproductions. There are two restaurants in the hotel, including the Port of Red Wing in the lower level, where cozy candlelight meals are served surrounded by the building's original rough limestone walls, and Jimmy's Pub on the fifth floor. Rooms and meals at the St. James are moderately to expensively priced. For reservations contact the St. James Hotel, 406 Main Street, Red Wing 55066 or call (612) 388–2846.

A second industry that drew national attention to Red Wing beginning in the late nineteenth century was the production of durable and attractive stoneware under the Red Wing label. Early in the 1880s three small stoneware manufacturing companies banded together to form the Red Wing Union and began distributing nationwide their distinctive ceramic water jars, jugs, pitchers, crocks, and dinnerware, all of which were made from local clays. Until it was eclipsed by more economical glass production techniques in the 1940s, the Red Wing Union's pottery was in such demand that at one point the company was the largest stoneware manufacturer in the United States.

Today there are several sites in town that give visitors a glimpse into the Red Wing pottery tradition. **Pottery Place**, the large brick complex on Old Main Street at the west end of town, was the center of stoneware production from the time of the building's construction in 1885. Now the complex is home to a series of factory-outlet retail stores, though photographs and displays offer some insight into the Red Wing Union and its operation. This building was also the site of the world's first tunnel kiln, and a small section of one of these kilns is on display to the south of the main entrance. In the **Pottery Salesroom**, located next door to Pottery Place, some of the original Red Wing pottery is sold, along with a large selection of glassware.

◆ **Redwing Stoneware Co.** is another point of interest for pottery buffs. Since 1987, when John Falconer converted a horse barn into a production plant and showroom, the traditional Red Wing stoneware has been on the rise once again. Visitors can meet Falconer at his new studio at 4909 Moundview Drive (2 blocks east of Highways 19 and 61) and see the Red Wing pottery revival in action. Incorporating the Red Wing Union's original glaze and color formulas, Falconer's exacting reproductions have attracted a widespread following. For more information contact Falconer Stoneware, 3572 Tyler Road, Red Wing 55066 or call (612) 388–4610.

The drive west from Red Wing up and over the wooded bluffs is a pleasant one through a pastoral landscape of gentle hills dissected by an occasional river valley. The same journey 500 million years ago, however, would have required a submarine, for at that time all of southern Minnesota was covered by what geologists call the Ordovician Sea—a warm, shallow ocean that stretched all the way south to what is now the Gulf of Mexico. Today evidence of the primitive marine life that thrived in that body of water can be found all over southeastern Minnesota, wherever selected layers of limestone bedrock have been exposed to view.

One such site for collecting ◈ **Ordovician fossils** is located in a roadside cut along Goodhue County Road 8, less than a half-mile north of County Road 9 and 7 miles west of the town of Goodhue. Park your car on the shoulder of the road, and with a good guidebook in hand, such as Constance Sansome's *Minnesota Underfoot* (Voyageur Press, Stillwater, Minn., 1983), start sifting through the gray-green rock fragments collected at the base of the exposed rock face on either side of the road. What you'll find without much effort will be fossilized remains of corals, sponges, and other long-extinct species of organisms. Some of these—like clams or snails—will look familiar, whereas others will send your imagination reeling in unexpected directions, trying to recognize familiarity in their shapes.

In the nearby community of Zumbrota, there is preserved a historic landmark from a far more recent era. Just north of town, in the center of a city park on Highway 58, sits Minnesota's last ◈ **covered bridge.** From its construction in 1869 until 1932, the 120-foot wooden structure, which is listed on the National Register of Historic Places, carried traffic over the Zumbro River. The bridge originally was part of the stagecoach route from St. Paul to Dubuque, Iowa. Perhaps harried stagecoach drivers were the target of the sign above the bridge's entrance that reads: $10 FINE FOR DRIVING FASTER THAN A WALK ACROSS THIS BRIDGE.

WABASHA COUNTY

It was a hot, hazy day in Lake City, during the summer of 1922, when eighteen-year-old Ralph Samuelson walked down to Lake Pepin, strapped a couple of 9-foot-long wooden planks to his feet, and shouted the immortal words, "Hit it!" With that, the sport of waterskiing was born. Waterskiing has obviously grown by leaps and bounds since that fateful summer day, but its humble beginnings are still marked by Ralph's original pair of skis, mounted on the wall at the Lake City **Chamber of Commerce** (212 South Washington Street).

Today Lake Pepin is still the center of excitement in Lake City, with countless sailboats, motorboats, and, yes, water-skiers dotting the surface on sunny summer days. A recently completed **walkway** provides strollers a good view of the lake. And should you work up an appetite on your stroll, **Waterman's** is an excellent place to stop. Located just off Highway 61 at the north end of town, the restaurant sits right on the shore of Lake Pepin and has an outdoor deck and an enclosed sunporch that overlook the waterfront. Should you arrive by boat, the dock out front provides ample parking.

Another favorite Lake City eatery is the **Chickadee Cottage Tea Room & Restaurant,** 317 North Lakeshore Drive (Highway 61). Modeled after a traditional English teahouse, Chickadee Cottage offers a delicious assortment of lighter fare for breakfast and lunch, including omelets, sandwiches, salads, and cheese plates. An afternoon tea, including scones, tea sandwiches, and various sweets, is served daily from 3:00 to 5:00 P.M. All-you-can-eat family breakfasts are offered Sundays from 8:00 A.M. to 1:00 P.M.

Three beautiful B&Bs in Lake City offer healthy doses of Victorian charm. The Pepin House (612–345–4454), the Red Gables Inn (612–345–2605), and the Victorian Bed & Breakfast (612–345–2167) are all located in the heart of Lake City, within walking distance of Lake Pepin. Just west of town lies Evergreen Knoll Acres, a 1920s farmhouse that has been turned into a B&B and decorated with antique and country furnishings.

Driving east on Minnesota Highway 60 from Zumbrota through Wabasha County is a great way to appreciate the special geology of the bluff country. Tight, winding canyons with walls of crumbling limestone and sandstone alternate with straight stretches of road that offer sweeping views of the pastoral landscape. As the Mississippi River approaches, the valley widens, the bluffs become more pronounced, and hillsides are covered with hardwood forest.

About 7 miles from Wabasha, in the midst of all this splendor, is Dumfries—a blip on the map that you'll pass in the time it takes to sneeze. In fact about all that remains of this tiny Scottish milling community is the hundred-year-old **Dumfries Restaurant**. This recently remodeled building served first as a post office and general store in the early part of this century and then as a saloon during the 1940s and 1950s, until the current owners added a restaurant with a reputation for fine steak and seafood.

A little farther east on Highway 60, just before you crest the last bluff and drop down to the Mississippi floodplain and the town of Wabasha, a sign will announce your arrival at the ◆**Arrowhead Bluffs Exhibits.** A half-mile drive on a gravel road leads to the farmyard of Les and John Behrns, who have built a monument to thirty years of determined collecting. For a small fee visitors can study examples of every Winchester firearm ever made, from the company's beginning in 1866 to the present. A total of 435 rifles, shotguns, and pistols are on display, along with seventy big-game trophies bagged by the Behrnses on hunting expeditions all over North America. Miscellaneous antiques and Native American artifacts are exhibited as well. Arrowhead Bluffs Exhibits is open daily May through December and by appointment the rest of the year; call (612) 565–3829.

If you have the opportunity to stay overnight in Wabasha—or if you have time only for a meal—the historic ◆**Anderson House** country inn is the place to stop. In continuous operation since its construction in 1856, this rambling, three-story brick structure is the oldest operating hotel in the state. Owners John and Jeanne Hall have garnered a national reputation for the inn's homey charm, for its very good Dutch-inspired cooking (the original Mrs. Anderson was from Holland), and for their renowned fondness for cats.

The Anderson House may well be the only hotel in American where guests can "adopt" one of fifteen felines for the duration of their stay. Other special amenities that have survived transition into the twentieth century include quilt-wrapped hot brick footwarmers for warming a chilly bed on a cold winter's night and an overnight shoe-shine service for guests who leave their shoes outside their bedroom doors. Specialties on the menu include Grandma Anderson's chicken and dumplings and Pheasant Jubilee, all at moderate prices. Reservations can be made by contacting the Anderson House, 333 West Main Street, Wabasha 55981 or by calling (612) 565–4524. (The restaurant is open Friday through Sunday from November to April 1 and daily during the rest of the year. The hotel is closed each January for renovations.)

For many people the Mississippi River, flowing slowly southward a block from the entrance to the Anderson House, is an irresistible attraction. If you're such a person—someone fascinated with the incredibly rich history associated with the river, a lover of waterfowl, an angler, or a river rat in the Huck Finn tradition—stop in at **Great River Houseboats**, at the Wabasha Marina, 1009 East Main Street. This is one of the few places in the state where you can create your own Mississippi River adventure in comfort and style. Great River Houseboats has several 48-foot vessels to rent in two models (economy and deluxe), each of which sleeps up to ten people. The boats are appointed with a full kitchen, a living room, a head with shower, a barbecue grill, and ample deck space for sunning and fishing. No special experience is required to rent a boat; novice pilots are thoroughly oriented before being turned loose on the Big Muddy. Depending on group size and boat, prices are inexpensive to moderate. Reservations should be made well in advance by writing Great River Houseboats, Box 247, Wabasha 55981 or by calling (612) 565–3376.

Capitalizing on the success of *Grumpy Old Men,* the 1993 hit movie starring Jack Lemmon and Walter Matthau, which was based in Wabasha (but filmed in Faribault), Wabasha now stages **Grumpy Old Men Days,** the highlight of which is an ice-fishing contest. For information regarding this event, which takes place in late February, contact Bonnie and Dave Koopman at Troy's Bait Bucket (612–565–4895).

Wabasha is also home to a large bald eagle population, prompting volunteers to set up **Eagle Watch.** Every Sunday between 1:00 and 3:00 P.M., from November through March, volunteers from town set up telescopes and binoculars so that visitors can catch a glimpse of these majestic avians, once on the brink of extinction but now making a strong comeback in these parts. Call the Wabasha Chamber of Commerce at (612) 565–4158 for more information.

Cruise 6 miles south of Wabasha just off Highway 61 and you will enter the magic kingdom of ❖ **L.A.R.K. Toys.** Opened in 1986 by Don and Sarah Kreofsky, L.A.R.K. Toys is a haven for lovers of the handmade wooden toys of yesteryear. The ever-expanding L.A.R.K. Toys compound currently includes an office building, a factory building, and a gift shop. In the near future it will also include a toy museum, a bookstore, and a gigantic carousel.

Eagle Watch

The highly entertaining gift shop offers an impressive collection of imported Christmas toys, tin toys, nesting dolls, handmade pull toys, books, and games. What's more, look carefully about this whimsical place and you may find trolls hidden in the rafters and large slingshots mounted here and there (used to propel the trolls on their nightly travels); there are even little mouseholes carved into the baseboards. Gip, the Kreofskys' pet pig, keeps a watchful eye over this fanciful domain.

The Kreofskys' toy factory is also a delight to behold, for it is here that the hand-carved characters for the carousel are being made. Sure, we've all ridden a horse on a merry-go-round, but who among us has ever ridden a dinosaur? or a moose? or a fish? You'll have to wait until the Kreofskys' grand carousel is complete for these experiences, but meanwhile it's quite interesting to watch these characters take form.

L.A.R.K. Toys may not be the Fountain of Youth, but odds are you'll feel just a little bit younger by the end of your visit. Catalog and ordering information are available by writing L.A.R.K. Toys Inc., Kellogg 55945, or by calling (507) 767-3387.

OLMSTED COUNTY

The city of Rochester repeatedly finds its way into the nation's headlines because of the Mayo Clinic—the world's first and largest private-practice medical facility and the city's largest employer. Perhaps it should be no surprise that most attractions in and around this city of 58,000 have something to do with the Mayo family, medicine, or both.

Free tours of the ✦Mayo Clinic leave visitors with the distinct impression of having passed through the Grand Central Station of medicine: The modern, twelve-story marble-faced structure admits an average of 1,000 new patients *each day* from all over the world. Sculpture and murals by prominent artists are found throughout the building, including, on the exterior north wall, an inspiring figure reaching skyward with outstretched arms by Ivan Mestrovic and, in a nearby courtyard, a delightful statue by David Wynne of a boy flying through space holding fast with one hand to the dorsal fin of a dolphin. For tour information contact the Mayo Clinic, 200 First Street SW, Rochester 55905 or call (507) 284-2315.

After a tour of the Mayo Clinic, culinary adventurers may want to explore the **Broadstreet Cafe and Bar**, a moderately priced, other-side-of-the-tracks bistro serving outstanding continental and American cuisine in a charming old brick building at the corner of First Avenue NW and Third Street NW. The Redwood Room, downstairs, has an à la carte pizza and pasta menu and live music (507-281-2451).

A tour of downtown Rochester's main attractions should leave no doubts as to the influence of the Mayo family on the world of medicine. But a visit to ✦Mayowood—the family's sprawling country estate, just west of town—reveals a flip side to the same coin that is just as interesting. This forty-room mansion, built into a wooded hillside above the Zumbro River, is a testament to the great wealth and social influence that resulted from the Mayos' successes in the medical field.

Mayowood lies at the heart of what was once a 3,300-acre estate of rolling hardwood forest purchased by Dr. Charles H. Mayo at the turn of the century. The stone-and-poured-concrete mansion, built in 1910–11, was largely designed by its owner, who also had the Zumbro dammed as a power source for Mayowood and to form a private lake.

The Mayo family presence is almost palpable in the mansion today. Among the numerous personal effects and furnishings is a collection of signed photographs and framed letters from former guests at the estate, and in these the Mayos' considerable social influence can be gauged. Just consider these players on the world scene: Franklin Roosevelt, Dwight Eisenhower, Lyndon Johnson, the king and queen of Nepal, Emperor Haile Selassie of Ethiopia, and King Faisal of Saudi Arabia.

Mayowood can be rented for special events, and scheduled tours are offered Tuesdays through Sundays for a modest fee by the Olmsted County Historical Center from April through October. For information and tour reservations, call (507) 282–9447 or write Olmsted County Historical Center, Box 6411, Rochester 55903.

Tucked away in a beautiful wooded valley west of Rochester, near the town of Byron, are a county park, nature center, and zoo quite unlike any other in the state. ◆ **Oxbow Park** is situated on 572 acres of an old farmstead around an oxbow bend of the Zumbro River. Ten kilometers of hiking and cross-country-skiing trails meander among the dense maples on the surrounding bluffs. The zoo, focusing on native Minnesota wildlife, doubles as a shelter for injured or orphaned animals, and the twenty-five species exhibited in tasteful displays include bison (buffalo), elk, wolves, a pair of playful otters, and an impressive group of owls, hawks, and eagles. Oxbow Park has picnic and camping facilities too.

On weekends staff at the nature center offer hands-on educational programs covering a wide range of topics. Each March, for example, there's the A to Z of maple syrup production, whereas in the fall you can learn everything you'd ever want to know about how to tan deer hides by using the animal's brains. Special events are held on major holidays too. The park, which is open daily, can be found 3 miles north of Byron and Route 14 on County Road 105 (the route from Byron is well marked). Admission is free. For more information write to Oxbow Park, Route 1, Box 170, Byron 55920 or call (507) 775–2451.

DODGE COUNTY

There is probably no town in Minnesota where the late nineteenth century is as alive and healthy as it is in Mantorville, the Dodge County seat. This unpretentious little community of 750 has been named to the National Register of Historic Places in toto. The reason? Virtually every commercial building to be found and many residential ones as well have been preserved and maintained in the spirit of the town's past.

A good place to begin a walking tour of Mantorville is the **Dodge County Courthouse**. Like many buildings in town, the courthouse, circa 1865, was constructed of Mantorville limestone—the industry that is largely responsible for having kept the community afloat since its founding in 1854. But unlike those of any other structure, the courthouse's walls are a full 40 inches thick. Perhaps this ample use of Mantorville's greatest natural and economic resource accounts for the building's survival as the oldest working courthouse in the state and the only remaining one that was built in the Greek Revival style.

Mantorville's other most famous landmark is the ◈ **Hubbell House**. This fine restaurant, which was also built of native limestone, has been in continuous operation since its establishment in 1854. The original Hubbell House served as a hotel for travelers who were passing from the Mississippi River to St. Peter. The guest lists reads like an eclectic who's who of American society: Dwight D. Eisenhower and Ulysses S. Grant represent past presidents; Senator Alexander Ramsey, two Drs. Mayo from Rochester, and Bishop H. P. Whipple hold up Minnesota's historical tradition; and from the sports and entertainment world hail Mickey Mantle, Roy Rogers, and the Ringling Brothers, among others. The guest register is prominently displayed, along with many photographs and documents of historical interest. What's more, the American-style food is good and moderately priced. For reservations call (507) 635–2331.

WINONA COUNTY

The county seat of Winona is a classic Mississippi River town—rich with history and graced with natural beauty—that has grown into a city. From the lookout at **Garvin Heights Park**, perched

31

atop the limestone bluff 500 feet immediately above the city, many of Winona's outstanding architectural attractions are visible against the backdrop of the twisting channels of the river and the Wisconsin shoreline beyond.

Among the most noteworthy buildings in Winona are two banks: the **Merchant's National Bank** and the **Winona National Savings Bank**. The ornately detailed, somewhat box-like Merchant's Bank, built on the corner of Third Street and Lafayette in 1911 by Purcell, Feick, and Elmslie, is considered one of the state's greatest examples of the Prairie School tradition. The National Savings Bank, with its huge pair of granite pillars looming skyward before the entry, is a fine example of the Egyptian Revival style. It was built by George Maher in 1914 at Fourth Street West and Main and, like the Merchant's Bank, boasts extremely beautiful stained-glass windows and skylights. The National Savings Bank also has an extensive collection of mounted African game animals that were hunted by a bank manager in the 1920s.

Although several interesting museums in town document Winona's booming development as a riverboat and lumbering community in the latter part of the nineteenth century, perhaps the most unusual among them is the ◈ **Polish Museum,** located in a former lumber warehouse at 102 Liberty Street. The museum claims to house the country's largest collection of objects from the Kashubian region of northwestern Poland—a contention supported by the fact that historically about one-third of the town's residents were from that part of the country. Poles who settled in Winona were largely members of the working class, and items in the museum document their life-styles through examples of clothing, household objects, and photographs of laborers, fishermen, and housewives going about their daily tasks. A Winona Wagon Works wagon recalls the westward treks once made by settlers arriving by riverboat. Also, the museum's close association with St. Stanislaus Catholic Church is revealed in the many religious articles that are on display. The museum is open several days each week free of charge (donations accepted) from May through October and is a site of great festivity each April for the Polish Heritage Days and in October for the Polish Apple Festival celebration.

One of Winona's less well known claims to fame is that of being the Stained Glass Capital of the United States. The nation's two largest art-glass companies, along with another smaller studio, are located in this town of 30,000. The second largest, ✥ **Conway Universal Studios,** offers informal tours of its operation at 503 Center Street. In this nondescript ex-grocery store you can see artists designing windows for churches and other institutions and workers scoring and breaking glass to fit the designs and then piecing the rich colors together with sections of lead channels soldered at each joint. Universal also works with the much-thicker slab glass and does a limited amount of glass etching using sandblasting equipment. Viewing the entire production process takes forty minutes to an hour. Visitors should call (507) 452–9209 to arrange for tours.

A visit to the ✥ **Bunnell House,** which commands a good view of the river 5 miles south of Winona on Highway 61, in the little town of Homer, provides some rare insights into the lives of several of the area's earliest pioneers. This Gothic Revival–style, three-story structure—whose white-pine, board-and-batten exterior has never been painted—was built in the late 1850s by Willard Bradley Bunnell and his family, the first permanent white settlers of Winona County. The house is well appointed with period furniture, suggesting a simple but quite comfortable lifestyle for the Bunnells and their children. But more interesting still are the lessons to be learned about its original inhabitants.

Willard was a Great Lakes steamboat captain and fur trader who apparently was on good terms with Dakota chief Wapasha, who gave him permission to build his home in Homer. Willard's wife, Matilda, was described by one contemporary as a model pioneer woman who spoke French, English, Ojibway, Winnebago, and Dakota, as well as several other Indian dialects. She was also a capable markswoman and canoeist, while remaining "lady-like and modestly feminine."

The Bunnell House is open for inexpensive tours Memorial Day through Labor Day (call 507–454–2723 for hours). A modest fee is charged.

The Winona Historical Society, which operates the Bunnell House, offers yet another perspective on Victorian life in the Mississippi River valley via a **Victorian Fair** held in early October. Food complements period music, craft demonstrations, fortune-telling, juggling, clowns, puppets, river cruises, and carriage rides. The Victorian Express, a 1907 steam engine–powered train with

The Victorian Express

deluxe and luxury passenger cars, has been pressed into service
for this event as well. Full- or half-day rides aboard the train can
include meal service and are moderately to expensively priced.
For more information call (507) 454–2723.

Another historic site of special interest is found 10 miles south
of Winona, along a tributary of Big Trout Creek on County Road
7 at the tiny town of Pickwick. Here in a lovely, narrow valley
dominated by steep limestone bluffs is the ◆ **Pickwick Mill,**
which, when constructed in 1854, was one of the first industrial
sites in Minnesota. The mill is an imposing, seven-story native
limestone building that was built with such fortitude as to have
withstood a tornado and a major flood. These facts are even
more remarkable considering that there isn't a single nail to be

found in the structure's beams, rafters, and floor columns—they are held in place by weight alone. Flour from the mill helped feed troops of the Union army during the Civil War; in the years that followed, Pickwick flour was also shipped to destinations worldwide. The mill is open weekends only. For information contact Pickwick Mill Incorporated, Box 645, Winona 55987 or call (507) 452–9658.

FILLMORE COUNTY

It seems impossible, but of the 10,000-plus lakes located in Minnesota, Fillmore County contains exactly . . . none. That doesn't mean, however, that there's no fishing in this part of the state. In fact the area's cold-water streams support native trout populations that attract anglers from throughout the region. A good way to find your way to the area's hot fishing spots is to call John Fishbaugher (that's his real name), a local fly-fishing guide who is happy to take out beginners and experts alike. John can be reached at (507) 467–3766.

The Root River, which flows west to east through the heart of Fillmore County, is one of the region's waterways deserving special note. The valley that it has carved is deep—up to 300 feet in some places—and forested with remnants of the Big Woods that once blanketed much of the southeastern part of the state. Wild turkey, eagles, osprey, and deer abound. And the towns that the river passes along the way—Chatfield, Lanesboro, Rushford—are charming and steeped in history.

Depending on the time of year and personal predilection, there are several ways to take in the splendors of this river valley. Minnesota Highway 16 follows the river from Lanesboro almost all the way to its confluence with the Mississippi River and is a lovely drive any time of year. In warmer months the Department of Natural Resources–designated **Root River Canoe Route,** which begins just downstream of Chatfield and runs for 90 miles to the Mississippi, is excellent for swimming and canoeing.

Bicyclists and hikers can follow the 35-mile ❖**Root River State Trail**—an old railroad grade that has been converted to a multiple-use recreational trail—along its gentle downhill course from Fountain (9 miles west of Lanesboro on County Road 8) to Rushford. The same trail is groomed for cross-country skiers in winter.

35

Regardless of your mode of travel, picturesque Lanesboro is a great place to begin or end any adventure in the valley. The **Lanesboro Trail Center,** in the lower level of the Lanesboro Historical Museum at 105 Parkway South, has maps and information about local canoe and bicycle rentals. History bluffs can acquaint themselves with the town's past by perusing the two floors of exhibits upstairs.

Stores in well-preserved nineteenth-century brick buildings on Parkway and Coffee Mill streets include the **studio** of local woodcarver John Thompson (100 Parkway South). The **Scenic Valley Winery,** located at 103 Coffee Street in an old creamery, has a showroom downstairs where bottles of Minnesota-grown raspberry, rhubarb, apple, and wild plum wines are sold, along with more exotic onion and green-pepper cooking wines. Visitors, who are welcome to sample the winery's wares, are likely to find members of the Brehm family hard at work with their handpresses. Call ahead (507–467–2958) to arrange for tours if your group is large.

With three moderately priced bed-and-breakfasts in town, Lanesboro isn't lacking in interesting places to stay, either. The flavor of a small turn-of-the-century hotel has been lovingly recreated at Mrs. B's Historic Lanesboro Inn (507–467–2154), though the building, circa 1872, was originally used by an undertaker and furniture maker. Five-course dinners prepared from locally grown ingredients are served at Mrs. B's Wednesday through Sunday evenings. The Scanlan House (507–467–2158), Historic Lodge Inn (507–467–2257), and the Carrolton Country Inn (507–467–2257) are the other choices for an overnight stay. And for dinnertime you may want to make a reservation at the restored Victorian House restaurant (507–467–3457), where authentic French gourmet cuisine is served nightly by chef Jean Claude Venant and his wife, Sonja.

There are two destinations just outside Lanesboro that outdoorsmen and -women will find interesting. The **Lanesboro State Fish Hatchery,** built around a freshwater spring at the site of an old mill just south of town on Highway 16, produces two million trout annually—nearly half the trout stocked in Minnesota waters. An educational slide show and self-guided tours are available free of charge.

Three miles north of Lanesboro on Minnesota Highway 250, signs point the way to the ◆ **Southeastern Minnesota Forest**

Resource Center. This small, nonprofit environmental education center sits in the middle of 900 acres of state forest on top of a spectacularly steep bluff overlooking the Root River. Excellent skiing and hiking trails radiate from the main lodge, which also serves as a great site for observing golden and bald eagles (up to twenty of the latter have been spotted in a single autumn day), wild turkey, and osprey. A tunnel, dug decades ago beneath the bluff to power a now-defunct hydro plant, has become home for the largest known wintering population of pipstrel bats. More accessible to visitors is a bat condominium, located at the center's main facility, which houses up to 3,000 of the fascinating nocturnal creatures. Also, tours are given of the country's largest shiitake mushroom–growing operation—the center's main demonstration project and source of income; the delicious mushrooms are sold here, too. The center is open year-round. For program information write Southeastern Minnesota Forest Resource Center, Route 2, Box 156A, Lanesboro 55949 or call (507) 467-2437.

Upstream from Lanesboro a few miles along the banks of the Root River in the town of Preston, many years ago a group of desperate prisoners tried to escape the Fillmore County Jail by tunneling out with their spoons. Although their laborious plan failed, today you would never be driven to such desperation— heck, you wouldn't even *want* to escape from the place—because the old Fillmore County Jail has been transformed into the Jail House Inn, an absolutely charming and most unusual B&B. Through much sweat and finance, the building has been restored to its original Victorian architectural style and graciously appointed, with breathtaking results.

There are twelve beautiful guest rooms, some with fireplaces, some with whirlpool tubs, all decorated with exquisite taste. From the hand-tiled bathrooms to the ornate wallpapers to the authentic antique furnishings, each room has its own distinct flavor. Some are named for their original function (the Sheriff's Quarters, the Drunk Tank, to name two), whereas others are named after their decor (the Oriental Room, the Amish Room, etc.). Perhaps most interesting of all is the Cell Block, which contains two queen-size beds, a shower, a bath, and the original iron jail bars.

Breakfast, every bit as tasty as the scrumptious accoutrements would lead you to expect, is served in a bright and sunny modern dining room. The entire premises can be rented, space permitting, for company retreats and other group lock-ups. Call innkeepers Marc and Jeanne Sather at (507) 765–2181 or write to Jail House Inn, 109 Houston 3 NW, Preston 55965.

Those seeking a more traditional incarceration experience may want to consider doing time at the Historic Wykoff Jail Haus. Located just 10 miles west of Preston, the Jail Haus was, until recently, an abandoned one-room jail scheduled for demolition. A group of concerned citizens realized that this would be a waste of a charming brick structure, so they decided to refurbish it and turn it into a bed-and-breakfast.

Touted as the smallest B&B in Minnesota, the Jail Haus accommodates just one couple per night, but guests have free reign over the entire structure. This consists of a combination sitting-sleeping room, a modern bathroom, and a "cell room," complete with the original iron bars and narrow bunk beds. The bunk beds have been fitted with cushy new mattresses, which, had they been in place one hundred years ago, might have made the area's more notorious hombres—folks like Jesse James—a lot less ornery. Breakfast is served up the block at the **Gateway Inn** restaurant. For reservations or more information, call the Bank Gift Haus at (507) 352–4205 or write to the Jail Haus, P.O. Box 205, Wykoff 55990.

Harmony, a sleepy little town a few miles north of the Iowa border, is unquestionably in the heart of farm country, and an unusual opportunity to become immersed in the pastoral life is made possible through a bed-and-breakfast network known as **Michel Farms Vacations**. Vernon Michel, himself an ex-farmer, works with a dozen of the area's grangers to arrange getaways that many travelers find refreshingly different. Some farmsteads are historic and furnished with antiques, others are clean and modern, but all offer a taste of farm life and afford a glimpse into the life-styles of the Amish living nearby in Minnesota's largest Amish colony. Prices are modest. Write Michel Farm Vacations, Route 1, Box 914, Harmony 55939 or call (507) 886–5392.

A few miles south of Harmony is a hole in the ground that has been swallowing up visitors for decades. The ◆**Niagara Cave** used to rate right up there with Wall Drug and Reptile Gardens as one of the most heavily advertised tourist attractions in the country, as a result of an extensive billboard and bumper-sticker campaign (the attraction used to have three kids working full-time on bumper-sticker detail). But highway-beautification laws in the

1960s changed all that, and now Niagara Cave draws a relatively modest stream of visitors who seek it out because they know what they're looking for.

The hour-long tour begins in the basement of the entrance building and quickly descends to a series of well-lit, horizontal passages that were cut into the ancient limestone bedrock by seeping underground streams. One of these waterways still courses through sections of the cave and in one place forms an impressive 60-foot waterfall that visitors can view from a suspended platform projecting past the brink of the falls.

In the cave, too, are many other interesting formations— deposits of colorful minerals, numerous fossils, impressive stalactites, and unusual eroded limestone shapes, some of which have been given cute names and labeled with placards by the cave's managers. There is also a damp little "wedding chapel" that, believe it or not, has been the site of more than 200 weddings. The entire round-trip hike is a mile in length and represents only half of the known extent of the cave. At its deepest point, more than 200 feet below the surface, the stream briefly reemerges into view in a room that is adorned with a fine collection of still-growing stalactites.

A modest fee is charged for the guided tour, which is offered daily from Memorial Day through Labor Day and on weekends during May and from Labor Day to November 1. The cave is closed November through April except by special arrangement (call 507–886–6606). Niagara Cave can be found just south of Harmony and west of Highway 139 on Niagara Cave Road.

Southeast of Spring Valley is a second cave system open to public tours. The ✦ **Mystery Cave** has known passages that total 12 miles in length. Tours highlighting the natural history of the cave are staffed by naturalists at nearby **Forestville State Park**, which now owns and manages the cave system.

One tour begins along the banks of the Root River at a spot where a portion of the river disappears underground—a common occurrence in this region of the state. Most of this cave is in the 400-million-year-old Dubuque limestone layer, a formation of huge blocks that results in square-shaped passages and large rooms. A second tour, starting at the Minnesota Caverns entrance, is mostly in the 500-million-year-old Galena limestone layer, which is characterized by high, narrow, irregularly shaped passages. In the Mystery Cave system are two brilliant turquoise lakes, as well as dramatic and colorful collections of stalactites, stalagmites, and flowstones (all of which are formed by water-deposited calcite). The Mystery Cave is maintained in its natural state (neither placards naming formations after familiar shapes nor wedding chapels are to be found), and the inexpensive tours, which begin at the state park, have a strong natural-history focus.

◆ **Thomas Meighen's Farm Village,** also part of Forrestville State Park, offers an immersion experience of a different sort. Park your car and cross the bridge to the farm village and you will be magically transported to the year 1899. The "locals" (costumed interpreters portraying Forrestville residents) are likely to strike up a conversation about the politics of the day or perhaps the bright future of the railroad industry. They will then lead you on an informal tour of the Meighen farm village, which includes a general store, a barn, a grist mill, an herb garden, and a home-stead, complete with office, parlor, and kitchen. Not only can you talk with the laborers as they go about their daily chores, you may even be asked to help with a little cooking, grinding, or gardening. If you're lucky, they may even offer you the going wage (about 25 cents a day).

The original community of Forrestville died out because the railroad went to Wykoff instead. Historic Forrestville, on the other hand, is alive and well and lots of fun. Admission is free, but a State Park vehicle permit is required. For more information on cave tours and park programs, write Forestville State Park, Route 2, Box 128, Preston 55965 or call (507) 765–2785 or, toll-free from within Minnesota, (800) 652–9747 (ask for Department of Natural Resources).

For several decades around the turn of the century, farms in southern Minnesota were worked by teams of farmers using gigantic steam-powered engines. This tradition is proudly celebrated today in the little town of Mabel.

Since 1960, Mabel has been the annual site of the Steam Engine Days festival, which each year draws some 35,000 people to town the first weekend after Labor Day. Because of the widespread interest in this event, in 1988 a ◆ **Steam Engine Museum** was established on the Steam Engine Days festival grounds. From May to September visitors can see various models of these huge iron workhorses, as well as classic and antique tractors, early gasoline engines, and several different evolutions of the threshing machine. Call (507) 493–5350 for museum times and for information on the annual Steam Engine Days celebration.

HOUSTON COUNTY

In the heart of Houston County, 3 miles west of the county seat of Caledonia, is a lovely pocket of wilderness encompassing a series of steep wooded ravines that dissect the valley of Beaver Creek, a tributary of the Root River. **Beaver Creek Valley State Park**, as the area is known, has fine hiking trails, trout fishing, camping, and weekend interpretive programs in the summer (for information on park programs, write Beaver Creek Valley State Park, Route 2, Box 57, Caledonia 55921 or call 507–724–2107). The park also has within its boundaries a unique anachronism: the only unadulterated, fully functional water-powered gristmill in the state.

Though it's within the boundaries of the park, ◆**Schech's Mill** is actually situated on the working farm of Ivan Krugmire, who still uses the original machinery to custom-grind feed for his livestock. The facility has been operating in this lovely little valley since the mill's completion, in 1876, by Bavarian master miller Michael J. Schech.

When visitors step inside the building's 2-foot-thick native limestone walls, Ivan briefly explains the history of the mill and sends visitors on a self-guided tour of the mill's upper two levels. Then everyone gathers around the millstones on the main floor, and Ivan sets the turbines in motion to demonstrate the New Process milling technique.

As the floodgates are opened and the heavy grindstones start to spin, the entire interior of the solidly constructed building—from the maple flooring to the heavy fir timbers far below—is sent into a shudder. Thick leather belts that run through the floor to connect wheels, axles, and wooden gears on different levels of the mill whir into motion. And the kernels of dried corn that trickle into a hole in the center of the 22-inch Diamond Buhr millstone are ground into a coarse powder. Tours are given for a small fee on weekends from April through October; call (507) 896–3481 for more information.

41

RICE COUNTY

The exterior limestone wall of the building housing the ◆Northfield Historical Society—a building that originally served this Cannon River town as the First National Bank—has the kind of rough and weathered look that you'd expect of a structure that's more than a century old. But closer inspection reveals some telling pockmarks that, to the residents of Northfield, carry a special significance, for it was here, on an autumn day in 1876, that one of the most famous bank robberies in Minnesota history was thwarted by a group of uncommonly brave citizens.

A visit inside the museum reveals the whole story. With its teller windows, vault, and account books open on the tables, the scene looks just as it did on that fateful September Thursday when three members of the notorious James-Younger gang strolled through the door to make an unauthorized withdrawal. Five more robbers, all wearing the gang's characteristic knee-length linen "dusters" to conceal their weapons, were stationed in the street outside.

Although the gang was accustomed to carrying out an operation like the Northfield raid without encountering significant resistance, on this occasion it was in for a surprise. Two citizens on the street who detected what was afoot gave out a call to arms, while inside the bank the acting cashier, Joseph Lee Heywood, refused to open the vault (which was actually unlocked). After a second bank employee escaped out the back door, taking a bullet in his shoulder as he went, the robbers decided to abort the raid. One of them paused long enough while exiting the bank to end Heywood's life with a shot to the head. Meanwhile, outside, a street battle was blazing.

In the end two townsfolk were killed in the fight, as were two of the outlaws. Several days later four of the remaining six bandits, who had fled westward, were captured or killed, leaving only Jesse and Frank James as fugitives of the broken gang.

Visitors to Northfield the first weekend after Labor Day can witness a reenactment of this event in the annual Defeat of Jesse James Days celebration. During the rest of the year, exhibits and a videotape at the historical society tell the tale. The museum, open daily, is at the corner of Division and Fourth streets; call (507) 645–9268 for hours.

Archer House

Though Northfield has calmed down considerably since the James-Younger boys were driven from town, there are still many interesting attractions for curious and adventuresome visitors. But first there's the question of lodgings, a question easily resolved at the ❖**Archer House.**

When this grand, four-story, French Second Empire–style hotel was built in 1877, the local press noted, "There is unequivocal indication of taste in every room"—a statement that couldn't be more true today. Owner Dallas Haas's loving renovation and redecoration in 1984 show unusual attention to details, as in the dried-flower bouquets, occasional antique household items, antique furniture reproductions, and strategically placed stuffed animals that highlight the distinctive shape and personality of each room. Even the smallest and least expensive rooms (prices are moderate to expensive) are amply comfortable, steeped in charm, and in many cases possess fine views of the walkways bordering Northfield's lovely Cannon River waterfront. Reservations can be made by writing the Archer House, 212 Division Street, Northfield 55057 or by calling (507) 645–5661 or, toll-free within Minnesota, (800) 247–2235.

If the Archer House sounds too civilized for your tastes, there's always the **Log House,** circa 1885. This intimate, comfortable, and quaintly furnished log-cabin-for-two is located just west of the town of Nerstrand, at the end of an unlikely potholed gravel road. Hostess Anne Mikkelsen and her husband, Mike, an artist, live next door in an intriguing earth-sheltered house, while chickens and sheep wander the grounds outside. Upon the arrival of her guests, Anne presents them with a loaf of delicious fresh-baked bread and a brick of cheese.

The wooded hillside and valley surrounding the cabin attract skiers in winter, wildflower and morel-mushroom hunters in spring, berry pickers in summer, and hikers in autumn. A brass sculptor who rents studio space from the Mikkelsens also welcomes visitors. Full breakfasts cooked by Anne—a former restaurateur—are included in the Log House's expensive rates; moderately priced dinners are extra. For reservations and directions write the Log House, 6575 145th Street East, Northfield 55057 or call (507) 645–2926.

Not far from the Log House are the studio and showroom of a soft-spoken, Minnesota-born potter of wide renown, **Charles Halling.** Wheel-thrown and hand-built pottery made by Charles has received regional and national acclaim; one of his dinner-ware sets is even in the Minnesota governor's residence. Best of all, prices for Halling's gracefully simple porcelain and stoneware designs start at less than $20. The studio is found at 11967 Gates Avenue, Northfield 55057 (telephone 507–645–6256).

If, for whatever reason, you find yourself beating a hasty retreat from Northfield into the sunset, you may want to do what the fleeing James-Younger gang did—stop in at the **Millersburg Store.** What was at that time a general store down the block from a hotel used by several members of the gang the night before the bank raid is now a lively saloon and restaurant run by Rose Hanzel. A few historical pictures on the walls recall the store's earlier incarnation, but the main attractions are the outlaw-sized hamburgers, criminally delicious ice-cream drinks, and the sprawling beer garden out back, which is replete with a horseshoe pit. The store is located in the heart of tiny Millersburg, 2 miles west of Interstate 35 on Rice County Road 1.

In 1826, knowing a good thing when he saw it, a French Canadian fur trader named Alexander Faribault set up a trading post for the American Fur Company below a rampart of high bluffs where the waters of the Straight River joined the larger-flowing Cannon. Business with the neighboring Dakota Indians was good, and Faribault eventually decided to settle at this picturesque spot permanently, building in 1853 the **Alexander Faribault House,** a Greek Revival design that stands today as the first frame house built in Rice County. Two years later the town of Faribault was named after its founder. Public tours of the completely restored Alexander Faribault House, located at 12 First Avenue NE, are given for a modest fee May 1 through October 1. Call the Rice County Historical Society at (507) 332–2121 for times and prices of tours.

Soon to follow Faribault's example was a German cabinetmaker named Carl H. Klemer, who in 1865 established a woolen mill on the banks of the Cannon River. Though in Klemer's time woolen mills were common enough in river communities like Faribault—his was one of 800 in the country—today the ◆ **Faribo Mill** exists as only one of three such operations nationwide and produces more than half of all wool blankets made in the United States.

Tours of the old mill are offered on weekdays (for information write Faribo Woolen Mill, 1500 Second Avenue NW, Faribault 55021 or call 507–334–1644) and allow visitors to witness the entire manufacturing process—from the cleaning of raw wool stock from all over the world to the dyeing of fibers in huge basement vats to the now-mechanized weaving process in a large room full of clattering electronic looms. The Faribo Woolens Factory Store (on Second Avenue just across the river), which offers blankets at discounted prices, is open every day except holidays.

In the heart of Faribault's downtown Heritage Preservation District, which includes two fine examples of Art Deco–influenced architecture in the **Rice County Courthouse** and the **Thomas Scott Buckham Memorial Library,** are several other destinations worthy of a visit. Wood-carver **Ivan Whillock's studio** is located at 122 Northeast First Avenue, just a couple of doors away from the Alexander Faribault House. Since 1962, when Ivan established his studio in Faribault, he has been upholding the Classical Spanish style of craftsmanship by working exclusively with chisels, gouges, and other hand tools to produce a variety of religious images for churches throughout the region. He also creates secular pieces, such as landscapes and wildlife scenes that reveal the visual perspectives gained by the artist during his early work as a painter.

The ◆**Cathedral of our Merciful Savior,** at 515 Northwest Second Avenue, holds special interest from an architectural and historical perspective. Hailed by architectural historians as one of the most impressive English Gothic–style churches in Minnesota, it was completed in 1869 as the first church in the American Episcopal Church to be built as a cathedral. Moreover, the structure's high vaulted ceilings were home to one of the most important religious figures in Minnesota history—the Reverend Henry Benjamin Whipple, the state's first bishop. Whipple, whose crypt is in the basement of the cathedral, was a great advocate of Indian rights. As a result of his intercession with President Lincoln on behalf of some 300 Dakota who were held responsible for deaths in the great Dakota conflict in 1862, 262 of the Indians' lives were spared.

Another highlight of a visit to the cathedral (tours can be arranged by calling 507–334–7732) is the lever-operated bell chimes, circa 1903, in the bell tower. Visitors are given an opportunity to try their hands ringing out a tune for the benefit of the long-suffering residents who live close by.

STEELE COUNTY

Except for the likes of Jesse James, most people aren't inclined to go far out of their way to investigate a bank that holds none of their money. The ◆**Norwest Bank** at 101 Cedar Street North in Owatonna, however, is one such institution that cries out to be visited. Completed in 1908 as the National Farmers Bank, this nationally acclaimed architectural treasure represents the most celebrated work of one of America's outstanding architects: Louis H. Sullivan. The cubelike shape of the building's exterior, adorned with huge arched windows of stained glass by Louis Millet, quickly earned the building widespread recognition as, according to one historian, "a jewel box set down in a prairie town."

Entering the bank through the low-hung entry, one is suddenly overwhelmed by the beauty of the interior. The arched shapes of the resplendent windows are repeated in lovely pastoral murals on two walls, whose earth tones blend harmoniously with the surrounding terra-cotta and cast-iron ornamentation that was built by the country's best craftsmen of the time. Though the building has undergone several renovations since its completion, these have been undertaken with a dedication to preserving the spirit and many of the details of Sullivan's original masterpiece. Brochures explaining the history of the bank are available, as are brief tours by bank personnel.

Another interesting historic site in Owatonna can be seen on the grounds of the Owatonna Tool Company, located at 655 Eisenhower Drive. Resting on a short stretch of tracks next to the old Owatonna Railroad Depot sits Engine 201, a steam locomotive that happens to have been the first engine ever driven by railroad legend Casey Jones. Tours of the engine for groups of five or more can be arranged by calling (507) 455–7000. Also, a booklet describing the history of the engine and the story of Casey Jones is available.

WASECA COUNTY

Before it was extensively developed for agricultural purposes, the heart of Waseca County used to represent the dividing line between the Big Woods to the east and the prairies that stretched for hundreds of miles westward. Today at this historic ecological junction is an institution that enables visitors to contemplate the changes that have taken place since the plows of the first white settlers left their marks.

◆ **Farmamerica** is an interpretive center that chronicles the evolution of the Minnesota farm from the late 1850s until the present. Visitors make this historic journey by exploring three different farmsteads: an 1850s settlement farm, a 1920s dairy farm, and a contemporary farm operation. There are also a prairie restoration area, a historic one-room schoolhouse, a blacksmith shop, and a church. From June to October, when Farmamerica is open each weekend for a small fee, interpretive volunteers occupy each farm site and illustrate historic farming activities. Festivals are held the second Sunday each month. Farmamerica is located 4 miles west of the town of Waseca on County Road 2. For more information contact Farmamerica, Box 11, Waseca 56093 or call (507) 835–2052.

FREEBORN COUNTY

Ever since humans first occupied the prairies of southern Minnesota, Albert Lea Lake, just east of the city of Albert Lea, has been a busy place. Following the retreat of the last glacier some 10,000 years ago, the shores of the lake were frequented by hunters surviving on large game animals. In the ensuing millennia the area's rich natural resources continued to support groups of nomadic small-game hunters and fishermen, as well as more sedentary, village-dwelling prehistoric farmers.

Those who would like to learn more about how these early Native Americans adapted to southern Minnesota's changing environment over the centuries would do well to visit ◆**Myre–Big Island State Park,** just east of Albert Lea at exit 11 on Interstate 35. Within this beautiful 1,600-acre sanctuary, three natural communities characteristic of the region during late prehistoric times—oak savanna, wetlands, and northern hardwood forests—can be explored firsthand. Also, the close proximity of these different natural environments creates a lush habitat for wildlife. Deer, several species of birds of prey, waterfowl, and white pelicans are plentiful, especially during fall migration.

Prehistory buffs will want to spend some time at the park's Owen Johnson Interpretive Center, where exhibits from a collection of 30,000 local prehistoric stone artifacts (one of the state's largest private collections) provide insight into past cultures. From the big-game hunters' exquisitely crafted large spear points to the hand-carved fishhooks of a later time, one can gain real respect for the ingenuity and craftsmanship of those whose technology depended on stone, clay, wood, and bone. Some of the stone knives on display reputedly hold an edge to leather better than any modern metallic blade. For more information about the park, write Myre–Big Island State Park, Route 3, Box 33,

Albert Lea 56007 or call (507) 373–5084 or, toll-free within Minnesota, (800) 652–9747 (ask for DNR).

Each autumn Bancroft-Bay Park in Albert Lea is the site of the **Big Island Rendezvous,** a gathering of groups dedicated to celebrating the life-style of the fur trade. Highlights of this event, which is held in early October, include a black-powder shoot, tomahawk- and knife-throwing contests, dancing and crafts displays, and a tepee village and trading post. For more information call the Albert Lea Chamber of Commerce at (507) 373–3938.

PRAIRIELAND

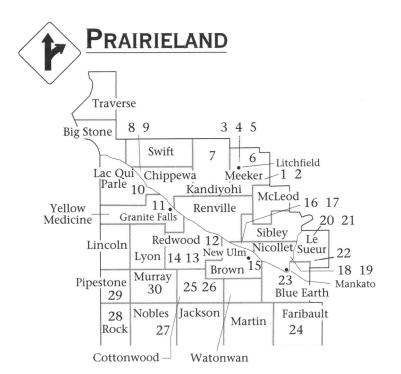

1. Old Depot Museum
2. World's Largest Ball of Twine
3. Birdwing Spa
4. Experience Agriculture
5. Grand Army of the Republic Hall and Museum
6. Forest City Stockade
7. Spicer Castle
8. Arv Hus Museum and Gift Shop
9. Karen Jenson's studio
10. Lac Qui Parle Mission
11. World's Oldest Rock
12. Lower Sioux Interpretive Center
13. McCone 1880 Sod House
14. Laura Ingalls Wilder Museum
15. Schell Brewery
16. Harkin Store
17. Fort Ridgely State Park
18. St. Peter Regional Treatment Center
19. E. St. Julien Cox House
20. Schumacher's New Prague Hotel
21. W. W. Mayo House
22. Geldner Sawmill
23. Seppmann Windmill
24. Riverside Farm and Studio
25. Heritage Village
26. Jeffers Petroglyphs
27. Nobles County Pioneer Village
28. Blue Mounds State Park
29. Pipestone National Monument
30. End-o-Line Railroad Park and Museum

Prairieland

Meeker County

When the first railroad train steamed across the Meeker County line on its way westward from the bustling Twin Cities in 1869, the first town it encountered was Dassel. The train screeched to a stop at a small wooden station, disgorged a few passengers and some freight, and then slowly chugged its way back up to speed, leaving a cloud of black smoke and ash in its wake.

In those bygone days—when huge steam-powered machines were transforming American life and half the North American continent seemed to many to be crying out for settlement—the railroad and accompanying telegraph service were the primary lifelines connecting little towns like Dassel with the rest of the civilized world. Today in this community of 1,000, there is a museum dedicated to the role that the iron horse has played in the history of many a Minnesota small town.

Originally, Dassel's ❖ **Old Depot Museum** stood in nearby Cokato. In 1985 the building was moved 6 miles west to its present site on the north side of Route 12 in "downtown" Dassel. Parked out front of the well-maintained wooden structure is a 1922-vintage wooden caboose that's been restored with such details as a coal-fired stove, a spring-mounted kerosene wall lamp, a real icebox, and a primitive "flush" toilet that could be operated in good conscience only when the train was at least a mile from the nearest town.

Inside the depot is a gallery of paintings and prints by Currier and Ives, Norman Rockwell, and others that captures the incomparable mystique of traveling by train to exotic locations. Another room contains collections of such railroad artifacts and memorabilia as railroad lanterns, signs, buttons, playing cards, uniforms, and dining-car china. There are also two delightful vehicles formerly used by track and telegraph-line workers: a velocipede (an odd-looking, three-wheeled-bicycle–like contraption that reached speeds of 20 miles per hour by means of a two-handled push-pull stick) and another one-person scooter, with bicycle handlebars, that was actually pedaled along the tracks. The museum is open daily Memorial Day through September for a small charge.

A few miles farther down the line, in the even-smaller hamlet of Darwin (population 282 by last count), there stands what is indisputably Minnesota's greatest monument to the archetypal human urge to collect: the ◆ **World's Largest Ball of Twine.** The ball of twine is only one of many achievements realized by Francis A. Johnson, who passed away recently at the end of a long life of collection. During odd moments in his career as a farmer, he claimed to have squirreled away some 5,000 pencils, 200 feed caps, and untold numbers of wooden ice-cream containers and paddle locks. Still, it was The Ball that elevated him to such heights of notoriety as being listed in the *Guinness Book of World Records* (which officially lists The Ball's weight as a staggering 10,000 pounds), *Ripley's Believe It or Not,* and Charles Kuralt's *On the Road.* Drive into Darwin on Meeker County Road 11 and see The Ball for yourself—it is slowly rotting beneath the water tower.

◆ **Birdwing Spa** is hidden in the heart of the farm country south of Litchfield—the next town west of Darwin on Route 12—though it's a destination that one would be much more likely to discover in the countryside of France or Germany. To find Birdwing you must zigzag around the edges of several large cornfields and kick up a couple of miles of dust on an unmarked gravel road that looks as if it's heading nowhere. Then suddenly a pair of commanding wrought-iron gates appear amid a thick stand of hardwoods, and you know at once that you've arrived someplace special.

Occupying the grounds of a lush country estate and hobby farm that was built in 1976, Birdwing is Minnesota's only full-service holistic health spa. Since 1985, when Elizabeth and Richard Carlson welcomed their first guests, people have been coming to Birdwing from all over the country to be pampered for two days, five days, a week, or more in a tradition that reflects Elizabeth's Austrian upbringing. Guests stay in nine graciously appointed rooms in a large English Tudor–style mansion. There are exercise and aerobics classes led daily by trained instructors, opportunities for hiking and skiing in Birdwing's 300 acres of lakeside forests, yoga and massage sessions, a sauna and hot tub, a fully equipped beauty room, and low-calorie gourmet meals. Rates at Birdwing are expensive, though they include all meals and services and are modest in comparison with those of most other spas. For more information write Birdwing Spa, 21398 575th Avenue, Litchfield 55355 or call (612) 693–6064.

Though to the casual observer the farms passed on the way to Birdwing look unremarkable enough, there's one that warrants closer inspection. Prefabricated metal sheds and modern field equipment are nowhere in sight, and without them the neat red-and-white barn and outbuildings, old cement silo, and turn-of-the-century farmhouse create the image of a farm frozen in time. That's exactly the effect that Don and Sonja Nelson had in mind when they began offering ◆ **Experience Agriculture** tours of their farmstead in 1987.

Don, whose farming career has included work as an agriculture teacher, saw the need to educate the public about the importance of agriculture and the dying institution of the family farm. Accordingly, he and his family restored their farmyard to its original appearance (except for the presence of the large red-and-white skateboard ramp used by the Nelson boys) and opened their doors to the public.

Visitors are welcomed into the haymow, where they can make themselves comfortable on a bale of hay beside a collection of antique farm implements that hang on the walls and listen to Dan introduce the state of the farm, circa 1900. Visitors are then free to wander through the active henhouse, the pungent silo, and the livestock pens, while interpretive staff explain how domestication and agricultural practices have evolved over the years. Kids get a special thrill out of romping in the hayloft, where Don has left several heavy ropes hanging from the rafters for swinging. A modest fee is charged to visitors, and the place is open to the public by arrangement. Organized tours are welcome, too. For directions, write the Nelsons at Route 1, Box 382, Litchfield 55355 or call (612) 693–7750.

In 1956 Minnesota's last surviving Civil War veteran died in Duluth at the venerable age of 106. Since his death, anyone wishing to visit the state's most enduring memorial to the War of the Rebellion has had to travel to Litchfield, where the ◆ **Grand Army of the Republic Hall and Museum** has proudly stood since its construction in 1885. Facing a large park in the center of town, the building's distinctive brick facade—replete with a large, castlelike half-tower in the center and small turrets on the corners—creates an unmistakably military aura. It is the only building erected by the GAR veterans' organization that is still in use in Minnesota and just one of thirteen in the country.

When visitors pass through the small entrance beneath a recessed portrait of Abraham Lincoln, they enter the original library, which now also serves as an exhibit space for a small but very interesting collection of items left behind by local veterans of the American Civil War. Most of the men who built the Litchfield GAR hall first came to Minnesota after the fighting was over to take advantage of the land grants allotted to Union soldiers in lieu of pay. Thus the stories generated by the museum's artifacts reflect the experiences of such famous fighters as the First Minnesota Volunteer Infantry, whose members led the decisive and near-suicidal charge at Gettysburg, as well as men from other parts of the country.

One exhibit case displays a leather belt whose buckle reads "CSA," that is, Confederate States of America. According to museum staff the belt was exchanged for one bearing the Union army's insignia when a pair of soldiers who had been friends in Ohio before the war confronted each other as "enemies" during a battle. On another shelf rests a photograph of a Minnesota volunteer who died of starvation in Georgia's infamous Andersonville prison camp. Elsewhere in the building a framed drawing of the camp depicts the desolate site at which 11,000 Yanks died of starvation and disease in the one-year period that the facility was in operation. Also on display are rifles and muskets, a pair of prized boots (many soldiers were reduced to wrapping their feet in rags), articles of clothing, and various personal effects.

The walls of the interior meeting room are hung with portraits of many GAR members, paintings of battle scenes, and original furnishings. In large letters just below the ceiling are rendered two proclamations: "In memory of our loyal dead" and "We are the boys of '61."

Adjacent to the rear of the hall is the Meeker County Historical Society Museum, which features items of local history. Both buildings, located at 308 North Marshall Avenue, are open Tuesday through Sunday for a small fee throughout summer. Call (612) 693–8911 for more information.

Though you might not guess it today, in the early years of Meeker County's history the little town of Forest City, 6 miles northeast of Litchfield on Minnesota Highway 24, was a community of some consequence. By the early 1860s enough bustling activity had been generated by a sawmill and flour mill located on the banks of the north fork of the Crow River that for a time the town was designated the Meeker County seat (an honor that was later permanently bestowed upon Litchfield). This explains why so many of the area's settlers simultaneously sought protection at Forest City during the panic that swept the countryside immediately following the outbreak of the Dakota conflict in late August of 1862.

On September 3 the settlers, using logs and lumber from the sawmill, hastily erected a 120-square-foot stockade around a two-story log cabin and barn, which now houses antique farm tools, circa 1860–1880. Today a reconstructed ◆ **Forest City Stockade** stands near the site of the original, looking much the same as the latter did more than a century ago.

Strolling about inside the enclosure's 10-foot walls, one feels a little claustrophobic, considering that this cozy space was shared for ten days by 240 men, women, and children. It was largely the women and children, however, who bore the brunt of this confinement, as many of the men ventured out to work their fields during the daylight hours despite the fact that the stockade was attacked the first night. Throughout the event there were no casualties—even a thirteen-year-old girl whose frightened family left her behind in the fields to find her own way to Forest City arrived safely at the stockade by nightfall.

The stockade, located just east of Highway 24 on the south edge of town, is open daily from mid-June through August. An annual Furtrade Rendezvous is held at the site the third weekend in August, featuring black-powder shooting, craft demonstrations, and plenty of characters camped out in 1860s regalia.

KANDIYOHI COUNTY

If it's a hot summer afternoon, one of the first things you'll notice upon your arrival at ◆ **Spicer Castle**—a grand turn-of-the-century bed-and-breakfast estate near the town of Spicer—is the breeze off the lake. Wander among the original furnishings of the spacious living and dining rooms, and then settle into a wicker chair on one of the surrounding porches with a glass of iced tea. You'll continue to feel the cool air pushed up the high, steep shoreline of Green Lake, carrying with it the sound of lapping waves.

This is one of the effects that John Mason Spicer had in mind in 1893 when he began building the six-bedroom English

Tudor–style home, which was originally called Medayto Cottage. The other consideration that steered this pioneer farmer, statesman, and developer of Kandiyohi County to this site is—as you'll discover yourself, if conditions are right—the lovely vantage point offered by Green Lake's south-shore bluff for observing the setting sun. When seen from the lake, the prominence of the stately "cottage," with its crenellated tower that protrudes above the roofline, prompted the nickname Spicer Castle, first used by fishermen in the 1930s.

In addition to the six comfortably appointed guest rooms in the main house are a log cabin and a cottage, originally John Spicer's office, on the grounds nearby. Rates at Spicer Castle are moderate to expensive. For more information and reservations, write Spicer Castle, Box 307, Spicer 56288 or call (612) 796–5870 or, toll-free, (800) 821–6675.

CHIPPEWA COUNTY

A walk down the main street of the little Minnesota River town of Milan, population 417, is enough to convince a visitor that this Norwegian-American community maintains an exceptionally strong tie with the old country and its traditions. Several wall murals depict Norwegian themes and locales, and the trim on many storefronts displays the work of Milan's two gold-medal-winning rosemalers (only four artists in the state have achieved this national recognition for their delicate and highly stylized painting on backgrounds of painted wood).

Drop in to the ◆Arv Hus Museum and Gift Shop (pronounced "arv hus") on Second Street to get a feel for the range of talents that the citizens of Milan have to offer. A gift shop of Norwegian craft items features samples of *hardanger* (embroidery), wheat weavings, pottery, and rosemaling.

In the back of the store there's a museum dedicated to the life's work of a local inventor, William Thompson, who in 1925 created a toaster-sized device called the radio booster that enabled rural listeners to pick up a dozen stations instead of only two or three. Thompson was also a pioneer in portable-radio technology. Wrapping 100 feet of wire back and forth over the roof of his Model T enabled him to boast of owning the region's first car radio. In the 1930s he built the country's first portable broadcast truck.

A block away from the Arv Hus Museum, at ❖ **Karen Jenson's studio** (104 Lincoln), visitors are welcome to stop by and see works in progress by one of Milan's top rosemalers. More locally generated artistry is also on display 1 block behind Jenson's home, at the Kviteseid Lutheran Church. A beautiful baptismal font with a rich green-and-red floral design was produced by Karen's brush, as were four playful murals in the church's downstairs bathrooms. The altar and pulpit paraments are handmade *hardanger* designs by another of Milan's artists.

Milan's folk traditions have developed such a following that a new folk school, **Milan Village Arts,** now offers weekend workshops and classes for those interested in developing old-world skills in weaving, silversmithing, painting, carving, and, of course, rosemaling. For information on classes call (218) 734-4853.

For Native Americans and European explorers alike, the earliest highway through this part of the state was the Minnesota River. Enough water flowed down the river to make for an easy passage throughout the summer, and the heavily forested banks offered shelter from the surrounding open prairie. Thus, when the area's first missionaries set out to begin their work, they had good reason to choose a place like the ❖ **Lac Qui Parle Mission,** found today in a wooded grove just north of where Chippewa County Road 13 crosses the river.

Lac Qui Parle was a thriving mission outpost from 1835 to 1854, serving a nearby Dakota village of 400. Of the half-dozen buildings that were once clustered together at this site, only a reconstructed church stands today. The towering cottonwoods surrounding the church and the exhibits inside, however, make Lac Qui Parle well worth a visit.

It was here that the Bible was first translated into the Dakota language in a written alphabet developed by the missionaries. Lac Qui Parle was also the location of the valley's first school and the first place in the state where thread was woven into cloth. During the mission's active years, there were a school, a corn mill, cabins for the missionaries, and a spring. Exhibits in the church, which was constructed in 1841, concern the work of the mission; the life of Joseph Renville, an early fur trader in the area; the archaeological excavation of the site; and the history and culture of the Dakota. The site is open daily, free of charge, during the summer. For more information contact the Chippewa

County Historical Society, Box 303, Montevideo 56265 or call (612) 269–7636.

YELLOW MEDICINE COUNTY

Granite Falls is a pleasant little city. It has an impressive park system, densely wooded residential avenues, and an attractive business district near the banks of the Minnesota River. The community's traditional small-town values are reflected in one of its historic sites: the Volstead House, at 163 Ninth Avenue, which was the residence of congressional representative Andrew Volstead, author of the bill that instituted Prohibition in 1919.

But that's not all, for just beneath the surface of Granite Falls's all-American facade, two of Minnesota's most exotic environmental features have been cleverly hidden. If you're a nature-minded sleuth you can unmask them both by parking your car at the Yellow Medicine County Historical Museum, at the junction of Minnesota Highways 67 and 23 just south of downtown, where a sign in the parking lot gives one of the secrets away.

◆ **WORLD'S OLDEST ROCK,** the placard states boldly. You peer behind it to see a lichen-covered clump of Morton gneiss (pronounced "nice")—a protrusion of gray, red, and black bedrock that probably looks no older than any other rock you've seen. But to be fair, when you're face to face with an object that's well over three billion years old, it may take a moment for its significance to sink in. Climb on top, make yourself comfortable, and give yourself a few minutes to think. Consider the sweep of monumental events that have occurred in the world since the time of Christ. Then imagine that if the entire existence of the rock beneath you were reduced to the scale of an average human lifetime, all that has passed in the last 2,000 years would have been experienced by the rock in slightly more than one second.

When you've had enough of such mind-bending contemplation, stretch your legs by walking west across the highway and into the woods that crown another outcrop of ancient gneiss. You have now entered the **Blue Devil Valley Preserve**, a thirty-five-acre tract of land set aside by The Nature Conservancy as one of the state's five natural habitats for an endangered lizard called—that's right—the blue devil. Also known as the five-lined skink, the blue devil is one of Minnesota's two indigenous lizards.

In fall and winter the quick little metallic blue creatures burrow into the crevices in the rock for protection. In spring and summer they tend to prefer cool, damp shelter, such as that offered by rotten logs and humus. Brochures on the blue devil can be found at the County Historical Museum, which has exhibits on local history and is open free of charge Tuesday through Sunday in the afternoons.

REDWOOD COUNTY

One of the big events occurring in the Redwood County seat of Redwood Falls each June is the **Minnesota Inventors Congress,** a gathering of creative folks—including children in grades kindergarten through twelve—from around the state who come together to spark ideas and to learn how to market and patent objects of their own invention. Prominent Minnesota inventors—both living and dead—are also recognized at the congress by being inducted into the Minnesota Inventors Hall of Fame. (For information about the convention, write the Minnesota Inventors Congress, Box 71, Redwood Falls 56283 or call 507–637–2344.) Each inductee is immortalized by the placement of a plaque in his or her honor at the Redwood County Museum, located on Minnesota Highway 19 just west of downtown; the museum is open afternoons Wednesday through Sunday, May through September, or by special appointment (for information call 507–641–8159 or 637–2828).

The historical museum occupies an imposing building that was constructed in 1908 as the county poor farm. Among a variety of local history exhibits is a room dedicated to the career of Richard W. Sears, founder and first president of Sears, Roebuck and Company. In the early 1880s sixteen-year-old Sears was employed as a station agent with the Minneapolis and St. Louis Railroad in the little community of North Redwood. One day a shipment of watches mistakenly arrived at his depot. Rather than return them to the manufacturer, Sears arranged to sell them himself to other agents up and down the line. The resulting profit spurned the growth of his famous mail-order business, which, by the time he retired in 1908, had achieved an annual sales volume of $50 million.

When Colonel Samuel McPhail and some companions set about founding the town of Redwood Falls in 1864, they had the good taste to establish the community around a beautiful wooded glen formed by the junction of Ramsey Creek and the Redwood River. The creek, named after Minnesota's first territorial governor, tumbles over a steep, narrow waterfall surrounded by pines. The waterfall soon became the focal point of this little oasis of forestland in the heart of the prairie. Today the 217-acre **Alexander Ramsey Park** is the largest municipal park in Minnesota.

A network of trails and roads winds through the rugged terrain, attracting hikers, joggers, cross-country skiers, and those who simply enjoy a drive through inspiring scenery. Also at hand are a zoo, an exercise course, a public golf course, two playgrounds, and plenty of space for camping and picnicking.

Although the history of the Dakota Indians is integral to the history of the Minnesota River valley, there are few sites in the area that provide opportunities for visitors to learn about the traditional life-styles of these Native Americans. An exception is the ◆**Lower Sioux Interpretive Center,** located within the boundaries of the Lower Sioux Indian Reservation on County Road 2, 9 miles southeast of Redwood Falls. Exhibits and films at the center provide an appreciation of the Dakota perspective of the events surrounding the tragic conflict of 1862. Visitors are also given an overview of the past 200 years of Dakota culture, from the time that the Indians were pushed westward out of the woodlands of eastern and central Minnesota by the Ojibway up to the present.

When the Lower Sioux Agency was built in the 1850s, it was one of two U.S. government administrative centers along the Minnesota River charged with the task of transforming the nomadic Dakota into Christian farmers. Despite opposition to this program by most Dakota, at the height of its operation the agency's population approached 100 whites and 3,200 Indians. There were stables, storehouses, a blacksmith shop, a school, a boardinghouse, and staff quarters. But by the summer of 1862, following a crop failure the previous year, the Dakota were faced with starvation. The gross insensitivity of the head agent—who refused to allocate food supplies held in storage and, through a representative, admonished the Indians to "eat grass" instead—was more than the Dakota could take. Tribal elders, moved to act against their better judgment by a group of enraged younger braves who had murdered a white family, declared war on the whites. When the fighting ended six weeks later, 300 settlers and soldiers had died, whereas the surviving Dakota (no one knows how many were killed in battle) had been either arrested or driven from their lands.

Today a stone warehouse that predates the conflict still stands behind the interpretive center, which is open free of charge daily, year-round. Call (507) 697–6321 for hours and information on special events.

Once you've had a chance to look backward into Dakota history, you may want to visit several other sites on the reservation that will give you a flavor of life there today. The sporting crowd can check out the Jackpot Junction high-stakes bingo and casino facility, replete with Las Vegas–style entertainment. Jackpot Junction is located a couple of miles west of the Lower Sioux Interpretive Center on County Road 2. At the Lower Sioux Trading Post, near Jackpot Junction, Indian-made pottery and beadwork are sold and craft demonstrations are given. And across the street in an outdoor staging area next to the community center, a large powwow is held in mid-June each year. For information about trading-post hours and powwow dates, call (507) 697–6185.

The lack of trees on the prairies of southwestern Minnesota posed an interesting problem for the area's first settlers: how to build a house? The solution most commonly reached was to slice up bricks of topsoil sprouting the ubiquitous prairie grasses and build dwellings made of sod. As strange as the idea may seem today, Stan McCone of Sanborn, in southeastern Redwood County, has proved that, properly made, a sod house is a downright comfortable place to call home.

Stan first tried constructing the ✦ **McCone 1880 Sod House** of second-growth prairie grass, but he found that without the extensive root system characteristic of virgin prairie, the sod just didn't hold together. Then he spotted an area of virgin prairie grass on an accommodating neighbor's farm and proceeded to plow up strips of the stuff with a special plow. After carefully stacking an estimated 300,000 pounds of sod in a cross-linked pattern and installing a wooden floor, rafters, six windows, and a sod roof (which he says weighs in at about 24,000 pounds), in August of 1987 Stan and his family proudly beheld their creation.

The 36-by-21-foot one-room "soddie"—tastefully appointed with two high-backed antique double beds, a wood-burning cook

McCone 1880 Sod House

stove, tables, chairs, and even a leather fainting couch—is as cozy as can be. Two-foot-thick walls keep the place cool in summer, warm in winter, and insulated from the sound of the persistent prairie winds. For adventuresome travelers willing to pay a moderate rate, the place is even for hire. Those just wishing to tour the soddie may do so for a token fee. To find the house, look for the first dirt road on the south side of Route 14, 1 mile east of Route 71. Stan can be reached at (507) 723–5138.

A pioneer alternative to the sod house was the "dugout"—a less labor-intensive dwelling built into an embankment or hillside that required fewer sod bricks. One famous resident of Redwood County whose family constructed a prairie dugout in 1874 was Laura Ingalls Wilder, the author of the popular children's book series on pioneer life that gave birth to the *Little House on the Prairie* television series. The site of the Laura Ingalls Wilder Dugout on the banks of clear-flowing Plum Creek is open to visitors for a small fee; it is located on the Harold Gordon Farm, a couple of miles north of Walnut Grove on County Road 5. *Little House* fans may want to peruse the Wilder memorabilia at the free ◆**Laura Ingalls Wilder Museum** and gift shop on County Road 5, just south of Route 14. Also, "Fragments of a Dream," an effectively staged pageant based on anecdotes drawn from the *Little House* books, is presented the first three weekends of July each year at sunset in a park at County Roads 18 and 20 in Walnut Grove.

BROWN COUNTY

The white community most heavily damaged by fighting in the Dakota conflict of 1862 was the eight-year-old German settlement of New Ulm. The fledgling city was attacked twice, on August 19 and August 23, and citizens defended themselves behind barricades erected in the streets. By the end of the two battles, thirty-four whites had been killed and 190 structures destroyed by fire. Indian losses were unrecorded.

Today, more than a hundred years later, New Ulm's strong German tradition is thriving. To find out just how much of a grip it still has on the town's 14,000 residents, drop in to see the **Brown County Historical Museum**—no doubt the only county museum in the state where exhibit labels are written in German as well as English. An interesting pattern of white-and-red brickwork graces the building's striking German Renaissance exterior, whereas the recently renovated interior of this former post office (circa 1910) has three floors of exhibits dedicated to local art and history. The quality of the displays and their contents is several cuts above that at most county historical societies. One whole floor is dedicated to the interpretation of Dakota culture, and the museum often displays paintings from a large permanent collection of works by nationally renowned artist Wanda Gag. The museum, located at the corner of Center Street and Broadway, is open for a small fee on afternoons Tuesday through Sunday. For more information call (507) 354–2016.

The Victorian era was a time when the construction of large public monuments was very much in vogue, and according to Minnesota architectural historians, in no place was that trend given such grand expression as in New Ulm. *Hermann the Cheruscan,* a sword-wielding, winged-helmeted Teutonic warrior whose stern visage has been looming above the city since 1897, stands in Hermann Heights Park (along Center Street on top of the bluff) as further tribute to the city's proud German heritage. The 32-foot copper statue of the Cheruscan tribesman who freed his people from Roman domination in A.D. 9 rests on top of a massive pedestal replete with ten stout Greek columns and a large dome. A circular staircase winds nearly to the top to afford sweeping views of the city.

The **Glockenspiel,** a large carillon clock tower on Fourth and Minnesota streets, is a more recent and decidedly less Wagnerian public monument in town. At noon, 3:00 P.M., and 5:00 P.M. daily, the Glockenspiel rings out a ten-minute concert, accompanied by the appearance of seven animated figures depicting aspects of the city's history. The figures slowly rotate on a circular stage midway up the 45-foot structure. On special occasions the thirty-seven-bell carillon is played manually as well.

What German-American town worth its salt would be without a brewery, you ask? The answer, of course, is none. And New Ulm amply fulfills this expectation in a beautiful wooded glen along the banks of the Cottonwood River at the south end of town with the ❧**Schell Brewery.** August Schell arrived in New Ulm in 1858 and quickly set up shop, rolling his first barrel of beer onto the delivery wagon within two years' time. His brewery survived the Dakota conflict unscathed (except for the unaccounted-for disappearance of two and a half barrels), and by 1880 Schell had outpaced New Ulm's other five breweries, establishing August as the dominant brewer in the vicinity.

Visitors to the Schell facility today discover that the *gemütlichkeit,* or congenial charm, of the place is arresting. From Memorial Day through Labor Day, they are free to wander through the lovely hillside gardens and beside the deer and peacock pens that surround a large European-style mansion built in 1885. The daily guided tours of the small processing plant, which produces only 25,000 barrels annually, are instructive for those curious about the brewing process. And each tour ends in the tasting room, where visitors can sample the eleven beers and sparkling beverages that the company produces. The brewery is located near the southeastern end of Franklin Street. For more information on tours, which cost a token fee, call (507) 354–5528.

Festival-goers with a taste for German culture may want to visit New Ulm during Heritagefest in mid-July or for **Oktoberfest**, taking place over two weekends in mid-October. Both festivals feature German food and music, including performances by New Ulm's acclaimed Concord Singers. At Heritagefest there are also a parade, running races, and traditional arts and crafts exhibits. For further information call the Chamber of Commerce at (507) 354–4217.

NICOLLET COUNTY

In the early 1870s the steamboat was the primary means of transportation for river towns like New Ulm. As the settlement of the prairies gradually resumed in the wake of the 1862 Dakota conflict, little communities up and down the river looked forward to years of growth and prosperity. Such was the case in the village of West Newton, 9 miles upstream of New Ulm on Nicollet County Road 21, where Alexander Harkin opened a general store in 1869.

Today visitors who drop in to the ◆ **Harkin Store,** where tours are offered Tuesdays through Sundays from Memorial Day through Labor Day, step back to that era of hope and budding economic development—expectations that were dashed for West Newton in 1873, when the railroad was routed through New Ulm, effectively ending the steamboat era, and when a devastating grasshopper plague wiped out crops. The Harkin Store hung on until 1901, when it was closed with most of its merchandise left intact.

Today 40 percent of the items stocking the shelves at the Harkin Store date back to the turn of the century, though visitors would be hard-pressed to identify anything inauthentic. In keeping with its former function, Harkin's store is a sociable gathering spot where news of the outside world, circa 1873, can be obtained from costumed guides and from notices posted on the walls. Evidence of the store's role as a post office, apothecary, and dry-goods, food, and implement dealer abounds. Coffee is advertised at 35 cents per pound, and bottles of Ayers Tonic promise relief from just about any conceivable ailment. Even the well-used checkerboard, whose hand-carved wooden pieces sit on top of the cracker barrel next to the woodstove, is genuine.

For information on tour times (a token fee is charged), call the Brown County Historical Society in New Ulm at (507) 354–2016.

◆ **Fort Ridgely State Park,** 9 miles farther upstream at the junction of County Road 21 and Minnesota Highway 4, combines fascinating history with a variety of recreational opportunities. The only Minnesota state park with a golf course, Fort Ridgely also has 11 miles of hiking trails, 4 miles of groomed cross-country-skiing trails, and 7 miles of trails for horseback riders and snowmobilers, in addition to camping, picnicking, and playground facilities.

The partially reconstructed fort occupies a prominent site on a bluff-top field that is surrounded by steep ravines. These natural wooded depressions sheltered hundreds of Dakota warriors during the two battles that took place at the fort on August 20 and 22, 1862. The restored commissary building, which now houses excellent exhibits on the history of the fort, military life in the 1860s, and the role that Ridgely played in the Dakota conflict, is the only historic structure that today appears much as it originally did.

Chances are that nothing at all would have remained of the small garrison had the Dakota decided to attack one day earlier, on August 19, instead of assaulting New Ulm, for on that day only twenty-nine soldiers were stationed at the fort, the rest either having been killed in earlier fighting elsewhere or being out on maneuvers to the north. The recruits who were on duty were almost all fresh volunteers with no fighting experience. But the extra day given the soldiers at Ridgely enabled them to boost their ranks and set up defenses for the attack that they knew was coming. In the end—thanks to the effective use of the fort's cannons, which primarily fired canister shot (collections of small lead balls that disperse when fired, like shot from a shotgun)— 180 greenhorn soldiers repelled 800 Indians while losing only three of their number. For more information about Fort Ridgely, call (507) 426–7888.

Each year in late June at Ridgely, the middle 1800s are brought back to life through the **Fort Ridgely Historical Festival.** Surrounded by more than a hundred tepees and period tents, the old fort grounds come to life with military and cannon drills by the historic New Ulm Battery, a fur traders' rendezvous encampment, folk arts exhibits, bluegrass and folk music, and traditional foods and beverages. For more information on the festival, for

67

which there is a small daily charge, write the Fort Ridgely Historical Festival, Box 292, Fairfax 55332 or call (507) 426–7840.

St. Peter, a Minnesota River community in eastern Nicollet County, is a town that has had to settle for second best. Following a well-planned, marginally ethical, and ultimately unsuccessful attempt to wrest the state capital from St. Paul in 1857, St. Peter was instead designated the site of Minnesota's first public hospital for the insane. Today at the ◆ St. Peter Regional Treatment Center (as the hospital is now called), which is south of downtown on Minnesota Highway 169, an interesting museum chronicles the history of the institution and the sort of care it has provided to its wards since the hospital's construction in 1866.

In contrast to many visitors' notions of the stereotypically primitive "insane asylum," when the state hospital first opened its doors it offered a variety of relatively humane therapeutic services in an effort to rehabilitate its patients. It was only sixty years later, during the Great Depression, that funding for rehabilitative treatment dried up and the hospital essentially became a warehouse for people who couldn't live elsewhere in society. Photographs on display from this period, which lasted until the 1950s, show huge dormlike rooms filled with beds no more than a foot apart. In another section of the museum, mannequins depict a variety of turn-of-the-century treatment methods, including early electric shock technology, insulin shock (whereby patients were sent into temporary comas with large and sometimes fatal doses of insulin), and hydrotherapy (whereby agitated patients were wrapped in wet sheets to dissipate their hysterical energies). Tours of the museum are by appointment only and can be arranged by calling (507) 931–7250.

Though never out of line enough to warrant a visit to the state hospital, the eccentricities of one of St. Peter's more colorful nineteenth-century community leaders, Judge E. St. Julien Cox, did get him into the kind of trouble that made headlines throughout the region. You can learn about the good judge's exploits by visiting the magnificent ◆ E. St. Julien Cox House, located at 500 Washington Street, a completely restored structure that one historian describes as the "most impressive example of a Gothic Revival dwelling still standing in Minnesota." The house and carriage house, with their high-pitched roofs, board-and-batten walls, tower, and round-hooded windows, were considered flamboyant by community standards when they were built in 1871, though they apparently were well enough suited to the tastes of their builder.

In the midst of an impressive career in public life that included leading a regiment from St. Peter to assist the beleaguered citizens of New Ulm in August of 1862 and serving as St. Peter's first mayor, as a Democratic member of the state legislature and senate, and as a district magistrate, Judge Cox ran afoul of his Republican enemies in 1878. It seems that they took exception to the usual etiquette in the Cox courtroom, which reputedly entailed sending defendants out for a bucket of beer before they were sentenced and staging miniconcerts—on a melodeon—by the judge himself, who was not above stealing an occasional catnap during moments of uninspired testimony. Cox was ousted from the bench following a sensational six-month trial that resulted in a whopping 7,000 pages of proceedings, only to be exonerated and reinstated a few years later by a Democratic-controlled legislature. Costumed guides relate the history of the Cox House and family on Wednesday through Sunday afternoons during summer and on weekends in September (for information call 507–931–2160 or 931–4309).

LE SUEUR COUNTY

John Schumacher, the proud owner of ◆ **Schumacher's New Prague Hotel,** describes himself as Minnesota's pioneer innkeeper. This "Minnesota German," who grew up on a farm in Wheaton, undertook the creation of his central European–style hotel in 1974, when the nearest bed-and-breakfast establishment was practically across the Atlantic. To this day his New Prague remains one of Minnesota's finest country inns.

A recently completed $300,000 remodeling project in the building—which was designed in 1898 by Cass Gilbert, architect of the Minnesota state capitol—has provided a more cosmopolitan touch to many of the inn's eleven guest rooms. Double whirlpool baths, built-in stereos, and gas fireplaces now accompany the hotel's traditional hand-painted detailing on the antique wooden furnishings and the down-comforter-covered beds.

The German and Czechoslovakian food served in Schumacher's three restaurants, inspired by John's extensive travels throughout the Continent, is outstanding. The hotel also has a gift shop featuring central-European imported furniture, glassware, lace, and linens and a lounge with bar stools hand carved to resemble the booted legs of a row of mountain climbers. Accommodations and meals at Schumacher's are expensive. For reservations write Schumacher's New Prague Hotel, 212 West Main Street, New Prague 56071 or call (612) 758–2133 (from the Twin Cities, 455–7285).

After visiting the ❖ **W. W. Mayo House** in Le Sueur, it's easy to see why rural Minnesotans in the 1850s consulted doctors only with trepidation and as a last resort. There were no licensing procedures for those who wanted to be a physician, no required course of study beyond several months of internship with another doctor, no minimum required skills. But as costumed guides at the 1859-vintage dwelling explain, in that era's hack-filled medical profession, William Worrall Mayo, founder of Rochester's famed Mayo Clinic, was an exception.

Mayo's upstairs examining room provides some insights into the forty-year-old doctor's far-reaching vision even at this relatively early stage of his stellar career. The primitive microscope on his desk, for example, is similar to his own, which was the first microscope to be used in the state. Meanwhile, the fully functional 1850s kitchen downstairs, which on any given day may well be exuding aromas of fresh-baked bread or muffins, re-creates the home life of the Mayo family. There is a gift shop, and a token fee is charged to visitors for tours, offered Thursdays through Sundays in summer; call (612) 665–6965 or 665–3250 for times.

A statue of two mothers and three small children engaged in a delightful dance stands in a little park adjacent to the Mayo House. The statue is known as the *Mothers Louise Sculpture,* and it is Louise Mayo, William's wife, and Louise Cosgrove, a later resident of the Mayo House, who, along with three of their children, have been immortalized in bronze. The Cosgrove family gained prominence in Le Sueur by founding the Minnesota Valley Canning Company—which eventually became Green Giant Company—in 1903.

A larger and more gracious home occupied by the Cosgroves later in their rise in prominence is open to the public as Le Sueur's only bed-and-breakfast. Pam Quist, owner of **the Cosgrove,** has preserved the 1890s ambience of this four-bedroom Colonial Revival house. The quality and extent of the woodwork

Geldner Sawmill

in the front hall and stairway are outstanding, and the rooms have warmth and personality. Pam's moderate rates include full breakfasts—Belgian waffles, Swedish pancakes, and breads—made of fresh ingredients. For more information or to make reservations, write the Cosgrove, 228 South Second Street, Le Sueur 56058 or call (612) 665–2763.

If the romance and imagery of the steam age—the ponderous metal engines, the billowing smoke and steam, the wide leather belts stretched great distances between wooden pulleys, the sweat and heat of the boiler—catch your imagination, you must pay a visit to the ◆ **Geldner Sawmill.** Rounding the eastern shore of Jefferson Lake on County Road 13 a few miles southeast of Cleveland, you'll find the weathered, shedlike building with a very tall smokestack on the west side of the road. Inside is a fully operable machine that played an essential role in the rural Minnesota landscape of the late nineteenth century.

71

The second Sunday afternoon of each month, May through September, engineer John Zimmerman fires up the boiler to raise the pressure in the system. Sawyer John Ballman and an assistant secure a hardwood log on the carriage, and the sawdust begins to fly. (The mill is also open for tours on the remaining Sunday afternoons throughout the summer.) This bustling activity is as interesting to watch as these men are enlightening to listen to.

As they describe the technical evolution of the machinery, the conditions under which employees worked, and the life-styles of the farmers who slowly cleared the big maple, basswood, oak, and elm off their land, a picture of Le Sueur County circa 1870 begins to form in your mind's eye. It was a place where the official dirt roads were often so impassable that most hauling of heavy loads took place on an informal network of "winter roads"—primarily the surfaces of frozen lakes. Thanks to places like the Geldner Mill, the log homes first constructed by the early pioneer farmers were gradually replaced by wood-frame dwellings. It was also a time when Minnesota's Big Woods were slowly giving way to the neat rows of crops that are found today. For information on special sawing demonstrations, call (507) 931–3150 or 931–5936.

In Elysian, the **Le Sueur County Museum,** located in an 1895 brick school building on top of the largest hill in the middle of town, is of special interest for art-history buffs as well as those curious to learn more about local history. Dorothy I. Hruska, the museum's director and curator, says that more than a quarter of a million dollars' worth of paintings, drawings, and prints are part of the museum's permanent collection. Among these are works on display by several world-renowned artists, including Adolf Dehn and Roger Preuss, who hail from nearby Waterville. These exhibits are complemented by a wide-ranging assortment of historic items: a 10,000-year-old skull of a now-extinct species of bison, 400 glass slippers, a large church vestments collection, and an exhibit dedicated to the work of a NASA scientist from Elysian who developed a meteorite detector for *Explorer 1,* America's first satellite to orbit in space. The museum is open Wednesday through Sunday afternoons in summer, weekend afternoons in May and September, and by special appointment; call (507) 362–8350.

BLUE EARTH COUNTY

The city of Mankato grew up around the confluence of the Blue Earth and Minnesota rivers, drawing its name from the Dakota word for blue earth, *mahkato*. The community of 43,000 occupies the slopes and floodplain of a broad wooded valley at the southernmost point of the Minnesota's run to the Mississippi. Each July the ten-day **Bend of the River Festival,** featuring canoe races, a parade, and other family activities, reflects Mankato's prominent position at the elbow of the long arm of the Minnesota. Two other annual convocations draw diverse visitors to this Blue Earth County seat as well. In late July or early August, football fans gather to watch the month-long **Minnesota Vikings Training Camp** at Mankato State University's Blakeslee Field. Then on the third weekend in September, hundreds of Native Americans and others return to ancient Dakota ceremonial grounds at Land of Memories Park for the **Mahkato Mdewakaton Pow Wow.** For more information on these events, contact the Mankato Area Convention and Visitors Bureau, Box 999, Mankato 56002 or call (507) 345–4519 (toll-free within Minnesota, 800–657–4733).

One of the first buildings encountered upon crossing the Minnesota River to enter the heart of Mankato's business district is an unremarkable structure with surprising historical significance. The simple, modern design of the **Minnesota Valley Regional Library,** located at 100 East Main Street, gives no hint that the site on which it stands is one of special importance to the history of the Minnesota Valley and the conclusion of the Dakota conflict of 1862. Yet it was here that thirty-eight defeated Dakota warriors were simultaneously hanged from a huge gallows in the largest mass execution in U.S. history. A statue of a sorrowful Dakota chief and a plaque commemorating the event stand outside the northwest corner of the building.

In the children's wing of the library, past the lobby's impressive boulder-filled fountain, is a special collection of books and memorabilia concerning Mankato-born author Maud Hart Lovelace. The Betsy-Tacy book series that Lovelace wrote in the 1940s and 1950s centered on her Mankato childhood, and many houses, buildings, and geographical landmarks mentioned in the books are recognizable around town today. Betsy-Tacy enthusiasts can visit the library to look through the Lovelace scrapbooks, listen to a taped interview with the now-deceased author, view a video inspired by the books, and chat with Shirley Lieske, librarian of the children's section and Lovelace expert. A Betsy-Tacy walking-tour guide is also available.

Not long after its incorporation in 1868, Mankato rose to prominence as an important center for flour milling and limestone quarrying. On Minnesota Highway 68, 5 miles west of town, is an interesting site that pays tribute to both aspects of Mankato's economic history. The ◆ **Seppmann Windmill** was built by Louis Seppmann in 1862 on top of a hill in what is now Minneopa State Park. The European-inspired conical shape of the mill's limestone base is pleasing to the eye, and its massive beams and burrstones only hint at the tremendous amount of labor that must have been required to build the now-inoperable structure. Thirty-five-square-foot canvas sails were supported by four huge wooden arms until the mill was afflicted by a series of natural disasters late in the nineteenth century: In 1873 Mr. Seppmann's mill was struck by lightning, losing two arms; then in 1880 a tornado took off two arms again; and finally in 1890 another storm wrecked the mill beyond repair.

Before leaving Minneopa State Park, you may want to visit a spectacular double waterfall, along Minneopa Creek (*Minneopa* is translated from Dakota as "water falling twice"). The 45-foot falls, which are a short hike from a picnic area in the southern part of the park, spill into a steep wooded gorge over a protruding lip of Jordan sandstone.

FARIBAULT COUNTY

The little town of Winnebago in northwestern Faribault County derives its name from the fact that from 1855 to 1863 a group of Wisconsin's Winnebago Indians, driven from their traditional lands by whites and by other hostile tribes, lived on a reservation nearby. Native American history and prehistory are the main attraction at the **Winnebago Historical Society** as well. From postglacial times—when this continent's first human inhabitants migrated southward from the Bering land bridge about 20,000 years ago—until the first contact between Indians and Europeans in the 1700s, the museum chronicles very effectively the evolution of the area's

Indian cultures in a changing natural environment. A headdress that once belonged to Chief Red Cloud and some beautiful Ojibway ceremonial beaded clothing bring the prehistory exhibit into historic times. The free museum, located at 36 North Main Street, is open weekday afternoons.

George Bassett is a farmer. He's also a nationally acclaimed sculptor and painter, and when you visit his ◈ **Riverside Farm and Studio,** 5 miles south of Winnebago, his doesn't seem to be an incongruous choice of professions at all.

George seems perfectly at home rummaging around in the old sheep barn and the other farmyard buildings that now house his kiln and cluttered studio. And when you study his lost-wax-method brass sculptures—especially the busts he made for the state capitol rotunda that have as their subjects Hubert Humphrey, Martin Luther King, Jr., and environmentalist Sigurd Olson—you'll find they have an earthy quality appropriate for a person who has spent many years working the soil. George welcomes visitors, as long as they call him in advance at (507) 526-2065.

A statue of a different kind awaits those who approach Blue Earth from the north on Route 169 near Interstate 90. Here, sporting a 48-inch smile and wearing size seventy-eight green fiberglass slippers as he gazes contentedly down on a new shopping center, is a 60-foot rendering of the **Jolly Green Giant.** The Minnesota competition for most kitschy roadside attraction is a hot one—what with the many manifestations of Paul Bunyan and Babe the Blue Ox up north and the various civic animal totems elsewhere. But whatever you may say about all the rest, Blue Earth's entry is surely the greenest—though from envy or inexperience (he's only been here since 1979) it's hard to say.

COTTONWOOD COUNTY

◈ **Heritage Village** in Mountain Lake is essentially a pioneer village—a museum built of a variety of transplanted historic buildings construed to represent a typical bygone town—but it's one with a couple of unusual twists. First, there are an extensive collection of historic telephone equipment and a general store that is stocked much as it was when it went out of business early in this century. Second, the area's Mennonite traditions are preserved in the **Heritage Ayte Shtade** (literally, "eating place") restaurant, located on the village grounds, which are found on County Road 1, 1 mile south of Minnesota Highway 60.

The inexpensive meals served by costumed staff at the Ayte Shtade reflect the fact that the Mennonites traveled widely throughout Europe in their search for social environments tolerant of their religious beliefs. Such Mennonite dishes as *moos*, a delicious cold fruit soup; *klups*, meatloaf patty with vegetables; and *perischki*, dumplings with fruit, reflect ethnic influences from much of northern Europe. The restaurant is open summer evenings (it's closed in winter) Thursday through Saturday and at noon on Sundays.

Though the experience is guaranteed to bring you rather abruptly back into the late twentieth century, there are two contemporary private residences in Mountain Lake that are well worth a drive by. Both were designed in the 1970s by architect Bruce Goff. The **Glen Harder House** is held to the ground by three large, irregularly shaped piles of stones that also serve as chimneys. Each of these is topped by a large sheet-metal cap with swept-up, pointy corners. These anchors are apparently necessary, as the house itself looks as though it's hovering a few feet off the ground, except at the corners, which are pulled earthward as if held down by spikes. The peaked roof has extended pointy eaves, in the style of the chimney caps, and draws attention to itself from miles around with its bright orange color. To find this creation, go south on County Road 1 from Minnesota Highway 60 just over 4 miles to County Road 13, turn east and go 2 miles, and then turn south on a gravel road, from which you can see the house.

The **Jacob Harder House** has been described by one architectural historian as looking like a "pregnant spaceship . . . sheathed in fish-scale shingles which really look more like chicken feathers." Looked at another way, this circular dwelling, with its two bug-eyed bay windows separated by a proboscislike bulge in the wall, just might be the visage of some extraterrestrial insect. Decide for yourself by driving down Eighth Street between Second and Third avenues.

Extraterrestrial influences may also come to mind upon visiting the ◆**Jeffers Petroglyphs.** There are nearly 2,000 rock carvings at this site, located several miles east of Jeffers and a couple

Jacob Harder House

of miles north of Minnesota Highway 30 on County Road 2. Each figure was chiseled into an exposed ridge of red quartzite bedrock at some undetermined prehistoric date. Together they represent the state's largest group of petroglyphs.

The circular trail begins at a tepee-shaped interpretive center managed by Minnesota Historical Society staff. After picking up a guidebook, visitors are free to wander the quarter-mile walkway, which is surrounded by virgin prairie, at their own pace. Many of the figures encountered seem to have been suggested by aspects of the natural environment, including animals like bison, bear, wolf, turtle, and elk. Human forms, sometimes wearing what look to be horned headdresses (perhaps similar to those used by Dakota medicine men in historic times), imply the possibility that at least some of the glyphs held spiritual significance. Others are simple geometric designs, hand- or footprints, or so abstract as to defy description. But whatever they may have meant to their creators, it's clear that making these figures required a lot of work. Each of them was pecked into the hard quartzite surface by a pointed rock held in the fist that was struck with a hammerstone.

The site is open daily free of charge during summer and on weekends through September. For more information call (507) 697–6321 or 877–3647.

Nobles County

Worthington's ◈ **Nobles County Pioneer Village,** more than most other collections of antique, historically furnished buildings in the state, has the feeling of a real town. Practically every institution that a thriving turn-of-the-century prairie community would have had is represented among the forty-seven structures. There's a law office, a hospital with an iron lung and a primitive X-ray machine, a train depot, a church, a millinery shop, two life-size grain elevators, a well-equipped schoolhouse, and even a doghouse. Enter most of these establishments, and the furnishings and artifacts arranged casually about create the illusion that everyone has just stepped out to lunch. Walk out on the empty street and you *know* you're in a ghost town.

The village, located just west of the Nobles County Fairgrounds, south of Interstate 90, is open daily in summer for a nominal fee. For further information call (507) 376–3125.

Rock County

Driving north from Luverne on Route 75, ◈ **Blue Mounds State Park** grabs your attention as soon as it comes into view. In a landscape of largely treeless, boulderless, and flat agricultural fields, suddenly you confront a ridge running at odd angles to the highway, as if a mountain were beginning to emerge from the well-groomed surface of the earth. Against a background of colorful prairie grasses you can see boulders and protrusions of Sioux quartzite bedrock, which up close are covered with lovely constellations of lichens and surrounded by clumps of prickly pear cacti. And as you approach the entrance to the park, a small herd of bison is visible in the distance. The sensation is uncanny: You've returned to the prairie of a hundred years ago.

Approached from the east, as they were by the westward-migrating settlers, the mounds appear bluish against the predominant prairie sky, hence the origin of their name. The face that the Blue Mounds presented to these travelers was a rugged one—a steep escarpment 2.5 miles long and up to 100 feet high, with a ragged line of oak trees at its base. Mound Creek, which flows along the northern edge of the ridge, has been dammed in two places to form small reservoirs; otherwise, little in the park has changed over the centuries.

Hiking trails follow the top and bottom of the cliff and meander across the top of the mounds, offering many vistas of the surrounding countryside and a chance to wallow in the rich prairie environment. Swimming is possible in Lower Mound Lake, and camping and picnic grounds are located nearby. The bison can be viewed from numerous locations. And at the southern edge of the park is an interpretive center containing exhibits on the natural history of the prairie environment.

Near this building is Blue Mound's greatest mystery: a 1,200-foot-long line of stones aligned so that it points to the rising and setting sun on the spring and fall equinoxes. No one knows when these stones were laboriously moved into place, by whom, or for what reason, though there is speculation that they may have been related to astrological rites of some ancient Indian people. For park information contact Blue Mounds State Park, Route 1, Luverne 56156 or call (507) 283–4892.

PIPESTONE COUNTY

The Sioux quartzite formation that gives rise to the geology of Blue Mounds State Park breaks through to the surface again just north of the city of Pipestone. But here a second kind of stone, softer than the quartzite and of a distinct reddish color, is visible too. It is called pipestone, or, after nineteenth-century itinerant artist George Catlin, catlinite. And the site now known as ◈ **Pipestone National Monument** has for hundreds of years been a sacred quarry from which raw material was obtained to produce the stone pipes so widely associated with the American Indian.

Despite whatever animosities existed between tribes, throughout most of its history the pipestone quarry was considered neutral

79

territory to which Native Americans from as far as 1,000 miles away would travel by foot and remove the soft clay stone in peace. Pipe makers still quarry and work the stone today, though since 1928 the land has been under National Park Service jurisdiction. A visit to the monument begins at the interpretive center, where a film on the history of the site is complemented by exhibits of pipestone artifacts, a gift shop, and craft demonstrations by native carvers. A $^3/_4$-mile footpath leads from this building through the quarry grounds. The trail winds through stands of trees (which have matured in the absence of the once-frequent prairie fires) along Pipestone Creek to beautiful Winnewissa Falls, which was formed where the creek pours over a quartzite ledge. Several quarry pits are passed along the way, appearing as gashes in the ground surrounded by discarded quartzite rubble. Notations chiseled into a trailside boulder are evidence of cartographer Joseph Nicollet's expedition in 1838. Even the bird-watching is excellent in this special place.

Pipestone National Monument is found to the west of Route 75, adjacent to the north side of the city of Pipestone. It is open daily for a small fee.

If you're interested in finding some distinctive overnight accommodations in Pipestone, the hundred-year-old **Calumet Hotel** is worth exploring. The handsome stone building, located at 104 Main Street, has a crenellated parapet and a large arch above the entrance. The Calumet (507–825–5871) is moderately priced and comfortably appointed with antique and antique-reproduction Victorian furnishings. A lounge and restaurant with inexpensive to moderately priced American food round out the offerings.

MURRAY COUNTY

When the railroad finally reached the town of Currie in 1901, it was faced with a little problem. Like many small Minnesota towns that were off the main rail routes but still large enough (or politically savvy enough) to warrant being served by the iron horse, Currie was at the end of a spur line. And, having made the 38-mile jaunt from Bingham Lake to the southeast, the engines needed some way to get turned around for their return trip.

The solution to this dilemma was to build a turntable—a section of track resting on a pivot upon which the engine and coal car could be swung around 180 degrees by the efforts of a single worker. When it was built, the Currie turntable was an unremarkable bit of engineering similar to many others of the time. But today it is one of only two still in existence in the state, making the ◆ **End-o-Line Railroad Park and Museum** an unusual attraction.

Once you're through marveling at how one puny human being is able to spin a locomotive as if were a top, there's much more to see in the depot and engine shed. The shed, which originally housed locomotives that weren't in use, is full of antique railroad equipment and memorabilia, such as a full set of section foreman's tools and a couple of track inspector vehicles—including the trusty velocipede.

Nearby, the depot has been restored in detail to its former glory, incorporating such touches as the strategic placement of a tobacco tin in the telegraph set to improve its reception. The building's two waiting rooms reflect a tradition of segregation by sex that was in effect until the 1920s. Under this Victorian arrangement, the men were able to spit tobacco and the women to nurse children without compunction or embarrassment. The depot's baggage room has been devoted to an outstanding HO-scale model train display that depicts the Currie railroad yards as they looked in the 1940s. Outside there's a restored caboose to be explored, the reconstructed Currie Store (the first general store in the area), and the region's first school.

The End-o-Line Museum is open free of charge daily during summer and by special arrangement at other times. For information write End-o-Line Railroad Park and Museum, Box 42, Currie 56123 or call (507) 763–3708 or 763–3113.

Lake Shetek State Park, 2 miles north of Currie on County Road 37, is in the center of what is commonly known as the Great Oasis—a lovely hardwood grove surrounded by a network of lakes amid the dominance of farm and prairie. Within the 1,175-acre park are no less than five small lakes and ponds, complemented by extensive footage on the shore of the much larger Lake Shetek. Thus there's lots to do for water-sports enthusiasts besides the usual state park fare of hiking, camping, and picnicking.

But Shetek is also a memorial site of one of the more gruesome encounters between Dakota and settlers in the conflict of 1862. Since 1987—the war's 125th anniversary, which was commemorated as the Year of Reconciliation—staff at the park have held an annual Shetek Revisited program over a late-August weekend to illuminate the complex tragedy that led to the killing of eleven settlers and several Indians at Slaughter Slough. The program includes a bus tour of sites related to this event. For more information write Lake Shetek State Park, Route 1, Box 164, Currie 56123 or call (507) 763–3256 or, toll-free from within Minnesota, (800) 652–9747 and ask for Department of Natural Resources.

RED RIVER COUNTRY

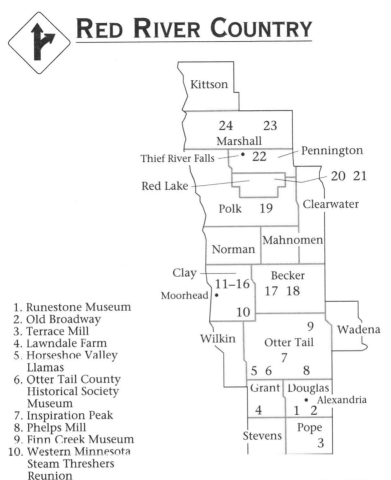

Kittson

24   23
Marshall
Thief River Falls   • 22   Pennington

20 21

Red Lake

Polk   19   Clearwater

Mahnomen
Norman

Clay   Becker
11–16   17 18
Moorhead •

10   9   Wadena
Wilkin   Otter Tail
7
5 6   8

Grant | Douglas
• Alexandria
4   1 2

Pope
Stevens   3

1. Runestone Museum
2. Old Broadway
3. Terrace Mill
4. Lawndale Farm
5. Horseshoe Valley
   Llamas
6. Otter Tail County
   Historical Society
   Museum
7. Inspiration Peak
8. Phelps Mill
9. Finn Creek Museum
10. Western Minnesota
    Steam Threshers
    Reunion
11. Agricultural Expeditions USA
12. Courtship of the prairie
    chicken
13. Bergquist Cabin
14. Comstock House
15. Heritage Hjemkomst
    Interpretive Center
16. Plains Art Museum
17. Soo Pass Ranch
18. Tamarac National Wildlife
    Refuge
19. Joe DiMaggio's
20. Red Lake River
21. Voyageur's View
22. Artco Corporation
23. Agassiz National Wildlife
    Refuge
24. Old Mill State Park

Red River Country

Douglas County

Standing in the middle of downtown Alexandria—an attractive town of 7,000 surrounded by numerous lakes and resorts—is a brightly painted statue of a huge Viking whose shield is inscribed with a brazen claim: ALEXANDRIA/BIRTHPLACE OF AMERICA. This dubious geographical declaration was inspired by an object housed across the street inside the ✦ **Runestone Museum.**

The story goes that in 1897 a large, flat stone with a long inscription of unknown characters was discovered entwined in the roots of an old tree in the nearby community of Kensington. The man who claimed to have found the stone, a Swedish immigrant farmer named Olof Ohaman, forwarded a copy of the inscription to a Scandinavian languages professor at the University of Minnesota. The professor and his colleagues, unable to render a translation of the script, concluded that it was a fraud. But nine years later a historian of Norwegian immigration, Hjalmar Holand, succeeded in deciphering the runic script and became convinced that the Kensington runestone is proof that the Vikings predated Columbus's journey to the New World by at least a hundred years.

Though the stone's authenticity has never enjoyed widespread scientific support, for some residents of Alexandria there exists not even a shadow of a doubt. A visit to the Runestone Museum—where the inscription is translated as describing the activities of a group of "8 Goths [Swedes] and 22 Norwegians" on an "exploration journey from Vinland [the East Coast] through the west" in 1362—will allow you to make up your own mind. The Discovery Room, where the stone is on display, features a video about the Runestone, as well as Viking artifacts. Other exhibits detail the more recent history of Douglas County, including a series of historic log and wood-frame buildings grouped together under the banner of Fort Alexandria. The museum is located at 206 North Broadway and is open daily for a small fee.

When you've had enough musing about the distant past, you may want to stroll south a couple of blocks to ✦ **Old Broadway,** a contemporary eatery in an elegantly refurbished nineteenth-

84

century home that offers outstanding food and drink. Normally you just don't find a restaurant like this in a town the size of Alexandria: The delicious nouvelle American cuisine is all made of fresh ingredients, and the late-Victorian decor is resplendent with imported antiques, including an ornate hand-carved hardwood English bar. In summer there's outdoor seating beside a landscaped garden. Prices are moderate, and reservations can be made by writing Old Broadway, 319 Broadway, Alexandria 56308 or by calling (612) 763–3999.

POPE COUNTY

When the flour mill was built along the banks of the Chippewa River in the little community of Terrace in 1903, there was trouble in the air. The railroad had passed Terrace by, and with it went the main source of hope and prosperity for Terrace's residents: a mill that had been built by the town fathers in 1870. The new mill was constructed in a doomed attempt to revive the community's economy.

After decades of observing a steady decline in population, the post office finally abandoned Terrace in the early 1970s and the little hamlet was threatened with complete oblivion. Then came a startlingly successful effort to restore the decrepit old mill.

Several times each summer, tens of thousands of people descend on ❖ Terrace Mill for some of the most innovative arts and music festivals to be found anywhere in the state. The internationally acclaimed Minnesota Orchestra has performed an outdoor concert, beside the wooden structure, that culminated in a stirring rendition of Tchaikovsky's "1812 Overture," replete with the firing of sixteen historic cannons. Minnesota's premier theatrical company, the Guthrie, has used the mill's portable stage and nineteenth-century atmosphere for such period productions as the Civil War–era *Red Badge of Courage*. Terrace Mill is also the site of an annual Heritage Festival Art Show in mid-June that showcases Norwegian-inspired rosemaling painting; classes and seminars are offered during the festival in this and other crafts. And each season ends with a concert in late August and an Oktoberfest celebration and Fiddle Contest the first Sunday in October, which draws fiddlers from far and wide.

Tours of the now fully restored building are given daily during summer (a small donation is requested). Terrace's Historic General Store has been renovated, too, and is now stocked with dry goods and gifts. Restoration of the miller's home and the town's original log cabin qualified most of the community for inclusion on the National Register of Historic Places.

For more information about events at Terrace Mill, write the Terrace Mill Foundation, Terrace Mill 56380 or call (612) 278–3289.

GRANT COUNTY

Herman is exactly the kind of quiet hamlet preferred by Minnesota's legendary stoic, hard-working bachelor Norwegian farmers. In fact, until quite recently the tradition had become so entrenched that seeing a woman about town was nearly as unlikely as spying a man without a seed cap. Then the national media decreed there was news in the fact that a town existed where bachelors outnumbered the womenfolk by evolutionarily suicidal odds, and eligible women began to show up in Herman's pool halls and taverns from as far away as Montana and California.

Upon their arrival some of these visitors discovered something else worth noting, namely, a bed-and-breakfast experience quite unlike any other at Gordon and Gay Ekberg's ◆ **Lawndale Farm,** 5 miles east of town. Granted, the sort of cozy accommodations offered in the Ekbergs' little two-bedroom wood-frame cottage—which was built by Gordon's grandparents in 1900 and originally sheltered a family of nine—and the delicious Belgian waffles served up for breakfast might be duplicated elsewhere. But the remarkable array of waterfowl from all corners of the earth that thrive in the farm's natural breeding grounds is rare indeed.

Fifty species of ducks, geese, and swans from every continent—totaling more than 800 birds—can be seen in natural-habitat pens and swimming about in an open marsh. Endearing newborns are hatched in large incubators, and guests are welcome to cuddle them in their hands. Surrounding the farmstead are hiking trails that wind through acres of restored prairie.

Some of the nation's top wildlife artists frequent Lawndale Farm to study and photograph such birds as the Siberian red-breasted goose and the brilliantly colored mandarin wood duck.

Prints by many of these masters are sold at the Lawndale gallery, located next to the guest cottage in a converted granary. Overnight rates at Lawndale Farm are quite moderate. For more information write Lawndale Farm, Route 2, Box 50, Herman 56248 or call (612) 677–2687.

OTTER TAIL COUNTY

Though newspaper magnate William Randolph Hearst, Jr., may not have been intending to start a trend when he imported the first South American llamas to the United States in the early 1920s, these graceful, woolly domesticated pack animals have found a fast-growing niche in American society. A visit to ◆ **Horseshoe Valley Llamas,** 3 miles south of Fergus Falls on County Road 25, gives travelers a sense of why.

A couple of dozen llamas serenely chew their cuds while monitoring with an attentive gaze everything that transpires in the surrounding pasture. They have long necks, skinny legs, dignified faces, and slender, curved ears that resemble bananas. Like their distant cousin, the camel, llamas walk with a peculiar lateral gait, swinging both legs on one side forward simultaneously. With one touch it's easy to see why their wonderfully soft wool, which makes the animals' bodies look much bigger than they actually are, is prized for making fine alpaca sweaters. Call (218) 736–4707 to arrange for a visit.

When you find your way back to Fergus Falls from Horseshoe Valley Llamas on County Road 25, awaiting you is one of the best county-history museums in the state. Exhibits at the ◆ **Otter Tail County Historical Society Museum,** located at 1110 West Lincoln, are laid out in a labyrinth of passageways that traverse the distance from early prehistory to the present—all within the confines of a single large new building.

The well-interpreted exhibits begin with the glacial events that helped give Otter Tail County its lake-strewn character. This sequence is followed by interesting displays on the Dakota and Ojibway, activities related to the fur trade, a scaled-down logging operation, and an impressive section on agricultural history that includes a life-size harvest scene in a shimmering "field" of real wheat. Victorian life-styles are displayed in a winding "street" of homes and diverse businesses, each appointed in detail with appropriate furnishings and artifacts. By offering such a fine representation of Otter Tail County's past, the museum, which is open daily year-round, also gives visitors a good overview of western Minnesota history. A small fee is charged to adults for admission. Call (218) 736–6038 for more information.

One of the pinnacles in Minnesota's less-than-alpine landscape is found about 25 miles southeast of Fergus Falls, near the tiny town of Urbank. ◆**Inspiration Peak,** as the conical hilltop is known, is part of what geologists call a terminal moraine that was formed by ice-age glaciers depositing quantities of sediment in a formation recognized today as the Leaf Hills. Along the wooded flanks of Inspiration Peak are a wayside rest and picnic area accessible from County Road 38 about 10 miles east of Minnesota Highway 78. Two asphalt footpaths ascend from the parking lot somewhat steeply to a clearing at the summit, 1,750 feet above sea level and 400 feet above Spitzer Lake immediately to the west.

The grand view from the top is well worth the half-mile round-trip hike. The Leaf Hills, covered with oak and other hardwoods, run in a rugged north-south line. To the east and west, rolling forest- and farmland stretch to the horizon. More than a half-dozen lakes are visible, and numerous grain silos reflect the sunlight.

In mid-July each year, artists gather for the Phelps Mill Summer Festival in the tiny town of Phelps, 25 miles northeast of Fergus Falls on County Road 45. At the center of this celebration sits ◆**Phelps Mill** itself, which is open for self-guided tours throughout the summer season. From 1889 to 1931 turbines in this well-preserved wooden structure drew power from the clear-flowing Otter Tail River to grind wheat into flour. Farmers brought their wheat to Phelps from up to a hundred miles away, often seeking overnight accommodations at the mill's "Farmers Roost" while waiting to collect their flour. The mill remained popular during the heyday of the Non-Partisan League, when farmers didn't want to patronize the large mills owned by "capitalists" in Minneapolis. Finally the drought of the 1930s brought an end to milling activities at Phelps.

Now the mill, which is complemented by a historic country store and log cabin, is part of the Otter Tail County park system. Swimming, picnicking, and limited camping are possible just

Finn Creek Museum

downstream of the dam. For more information about the park and the arts festival, write the Fergus Falls Chamber of Commerce, 202 South Court Street, Fergus Falls 56537 or call (218) 736–6951.

One of the ethnic groups well represented in eastern Otter Tail County is the Finns, and a good place to explore their heritage is ◆ **Finn Creek Museum,** found off Minnesota Highway 106 about 3 miles southeast of New York Mills (look for signs on Highway 106). The museum consists of a complete farmstead that was built by Siffert and Wilhelmiina Tapio in 1900.

The family's house—originally a one-room log building that was later expanded and covered with wood siding—is furnished much as it would have been at the turn of the century. A hand pump supplies water in the kitchen, woodstoves heat each room, and straw mattresses cover the beds, including one on an adjacent porch that was slept in by a tuberculosis-afflicted daughter whose treatment called for lots of fresh air. Among the many smaller household items displayed is a sinister-looking collection of bloodletting equipment, including a razorlike instrument for making incisions and several hollowed-out animal horns that were sucked on to draw blood.

Outside there's a well with a large hand-hewn beam serving as a counterbalance to the bucket—an arrangement known in Finnish as a *vintti kaivo.* Other buildings include a blacksmith shop, two small barns full of historic farm implements, a summer kitchen, and two log saunas, one of which is roofed in birchbark and called a *savu,* or smoke, sauna. This building was heated by a chimneyless woodstove. Once the rocks surrounding the stove were hot, the building was aired out and used for its intended purposes—which included birthing babies.

An annual Summer Folk Festival, celebrating Finnish culture with traditional music, craft demonstrations, and food, is held at Finn Creek the fourth weekend in August. A slight fee is charged for this event; otherwise, the museum, which is open afternoons in summer, charges no admission.

CLAY COUNTY

Not far over the Otter Trail County line on Minnesota Highway 32 is a tiny hamlet called Rollag, which consists primarily of three institutions. First is the **Rollag Store,** a wooden structure with peeling paint that is set back into the bushes next to an ancient kerosene pump. This quintessential general store provides its community with just about anything anyone could want that isn't found at Rollag's second institution: a large and thoroughly modern farm-implement dealership. Finally, just north of "downtown" on a dusty hilltop is a sprawling collection of mismatched buildings, unrecognizable pieces of heavy iron machinery, and a couple of steam railroad engines that seem, by the lay of the tracks, to go no place special.

On Labor Day weekend each year, this ghost town, known locally as Threshermen's Hill, comes roaring to life for the ♦ **Western Minnesota Steam Threshers Reunion,** an event that some claim is the largest gathering of steam-engine enthusiasts in the world (that's what they'll tell you at the Rollag Store, anyway). In truth up to 80,000 people converge on little Rollag for a celebration that includes just about every artifact ever made that ran on steam. There are stream threshers, of course, three steam-powered "Trains to Nowhere," merry-go-rounds that run on steam, steam-powered sawmills, and several monstrous steam engines with whirring flywheels up to 17 feet in diameter. There are also more than a hundred antique tractors engaged in pulling matches, a pioneer farm, an antique flour mill, traditional craft demonstrations, style shows of long-outdated fashions, threshermen's breakfasts, and a fiddlers' jamboree each evening.

There is a modest fee for adults to participate in this gala festival; for children, it's free. For more information contact Stan Grothe, 720 North Tenth Street, Hawley 56549.

Driving from Rollag toward Moorhead, it is impossible to escape noticing how very flat the landscape becomes—a sign that you've entered the valley of the Red River of the North. The river's flood-plain has some of the most fertile agricultural land on earth. And for those who are interested in learning how modern-day farmers work the land in this area, three-hour farm tours are offered through ◆ **Agricultural Expeditions USA,** a program of the Fargo-Moorhead Convention and Visitor's Bureau. These tours, scheduled weekday mornings Memorial Day through Labor Day, involve a visit to one of the area's 2,000-acre family-owned dairy or sugar-beet farms and a tour of an agricultural products processing plant. Reservations, which should be secured at least a day in advance, can be made by calling the visitor's bureau at (701) 237–6134 or, toll-free from within Minnesota, (800) 235–7654.

Despite the fact that almost anywhere you look in the Red River valley you'll see row after row of crops running toward the horizon, not quite all the land around Moorhead is dedicated to farming. Here and there, patches of restored prairie have been maintained, partly in an effort to preserve environmental enclaves for the performance of one of the most unusual spectacles to be witnessed in Minnesota's animal kingdom.

The ◆ **courtship of the prairie chicken** is a fascinating annual event in these parts that, to be honest, demands certain rigors of those who want to see it. Having made the necessary arrangements well beforehand, you must arise an hour or so before dawn and find your way to a "blind"—a cubelike canvas tent staked securely to the ground—somewhere in the middle of a field that seems as big as the endless prairie sky. Then you

Chicken Blind

sit tight and wait. If all goes well (and it usually does if the blind is well placed), about a half-hour before sunrise the chickens will begin stirring.

Probably before you can see anything at all, you'll hear a peculiar deep-throated whooping sound that hits three distinct notes. This is the "booming" that these birds are so well known for. When making this sound, the male chickens lift up special pinnae (feathers) on the backs of their necks into a vertical position while inflating the bright yellow air bags that the feathers normally hide; thus posed, in the dim light they could be mistaken for jowly rabbits. The booming, which is given off as the air bags deflate, is often followed by some frantic foot stomping, complete with appropriate sound effects of a sudden leap into the air, usually performed in tandem by two males against each other in a head-to-head duel.

These histrionics are accompanied by a wide range of other noises, resembling, among other things, tropical bird calls, meows, the cooing of pigeons, an old woman's cackle, and an infant's forlorn crying. What all this means exactly no one is sure; however, the general scenario to which you are a witness has to do with each male defending his oval breeding territory against other males while trying to attract the amorous attention of any females in the vicinity.

Once they get started, the chickens usually occupy themselves in this way for two or three hours, providing plenty of opportunities for you to preserve it all on film if you like. Active season on the booming grounds begins in late March and runs through April. For more information contact Brian Winter, a representative of the Nature Conservancy, Route 2, Box 240, Glyndon 56547 (218–498–2679).

Two historic sites in Moorhead offer visitors distinctly different views of the community's early history. The first is the ◆ **Bergquist Cabin,** Moorhead's oldest permanent dwelling, which is located in a wooded glade on the banks of the Red River of the North. A small log building with simple period furnishings, the cabin accurately conveys the humble beginnings of its remarkable builder.

John G. Bergquist decided to leave Smaland, Sweden, for the New World in 1868 after receiving a severe beating from his father for having been caught playing a forbidden musical instrument, an accordion, in the woods near his home. He traveled westward by rail to Brainerd and then set out alone on foot, first to a land office in Alexandria and then northwest along the Red River Trail to what was eventually to become Moorhead. He arrived in the Red River valley in midwinter and took shelter in the only building within sight—an abandoned stagecoach stop, which he shared with a fellow traveler who spoke only English. John, whose sole tongue was Swedish, undertook all this at the tender age of eighteen.

The following summer, in 1870, he built his cabin and set up a modest farm. Within five years the town was beginning to take shape around him, and he eventually started a successful brick manufacturing business, using the clay he found in the riverbank near his home. Tours of the Bergquist Cabin, which is found on a dirt road near the west end of Eleventh Avenue, can be arranged by contacting the Clay County Historical Society; call (218) 233–4604.

The ◆ **Comstock House,** at 506 Eighth Street South, is a well-preserved example of the kind of society to which the likes of John Bergquist might have aspired. Solomon G. Comstock built this gracious, eleven-room, Queen Anne–style home—whose foundation was provided by the Bergquist brickworks—in 1883 after having established himself as one of the community's most prominent residents. During a sixty-year public career, Solomon served Moorhead as the Clay County attorney, a state representative and senator, and a member of the Fifty-seventh Congress. His relationship with railroad baron James J. Hill helped secure an extensive railroad system in the Red River valley. And he was pivotal in the establishment of a state normal school in Moorhead, which later became Moorhead State College.

Owned and maintained by the Minnesota Historical Society, the Comstock House is replete with most of the family's original furnishings, reflecting a well-to-do life-style that nevertheless falls short of the opulence found in some grand homes elsewhere in the state. The house is open to the public for a small fee on weekends in summer and by appointment at other times. Call (218) 233–0848 for more information.

Not far from the Bergquist Cabin, in a wooded park on the banks of the Red River, is a monument that stands quite literally in recognition of a dream come true. With its high-peaked twin towers and white tentlike shape, it even looks a little dreamy. But the ◆ **Heritage Hjemkomst Interpretive Center** is real enough, as is the magnificent wooden vessel within it.

Hjemkomst (pronounced "yemkomst") means "homecoming" in Norwegian, and it was the vision of paying a dramatic tribute to the seafaring Vikings of his homeland that inspired a local teacher, Robert Asp, to begin work in 1971 on a project that dominated the last years of his life. His plan was to build an authentic Viking sailing ship, the *Hjemkomst,* and to sail it from Duluth to Norway. It was nine years before Robert was able to stand at the ship's helm on its maiden voyage in Duluth harbor, and not long afterward he died of leukemia. But several members of his family saw his dream through to fruition, landing the *Hjemkomst* in Bergen, Norway, on July 19, 1982.

The multimillion-dollar interpretive center that has been built in the *Hjemkomst*'s honor is an impressive site. Beneath the building's steeply pitched fiberglass roof, the ship is displayed fully rigged, along with many artifacts associated with its construction and sailing. The well-interpreted displays are complemented by a moving twenty-minute documentary, shown in an adjacent auditorium, on the construction and voyage of the *Hjemkomst*. In addition to this exhibit are a large space for traveling exhibitions and a gallery for items from the Clay County Historical Museum's permanent collection. The Heritage Hjemkomst Interpretive Center is open daily year-round for a small fee (for information on special exhibits, call 218–233–5604). It can be found at 202 First Avenue North.

A visit to the ◆ **Plains Art Museum** in Moorhead quickly reveals the lie behind the common misconception that cultural life in rural Minnesota is as arid as the land is flat. Occupying two floors of a historic building—formerly the Moorhead Post Office—the museum displays works by prominent contemporary artists who have been professionally or personally associated with the upper Midwest. The influence of the northern plains environment is evident in some paintings in the permanent collection, as are historic and cultural themes expressed by Dakota and Ojibway artists. A large gallery downstairs provides space for traveling exhibits. The Plains Art Museum, located at 512 Main Avenue, is open Tuesday through Saturday year-round. Admission is free.

BECKER COUNTY

Besides being a popular summer vacation spot, the Becker County seat of Detroit Lakes happens to be the annual site of the Midwest's largest country-and-western music festival. During the WE Fest, held the first weekend in August, the likes of Waylon Jennings and Willie Nelson get together with many of their star-studded buddies for three days of outdoor music and fun.

The ◆ **Soo Pass Ranch,** 3 miles south of Detroit Lakes on Route 59, is where it all happens. Campgrounds at the ranch, including one just for families, provide space for 5,000 campers. A rock-and-roll Fourth of July celebration called Celebrate America is also held at the ranch each year. Tickets and camping reservations for the WE Fest and Celebrate America, which start at about $70 per person, can be ordered by mail (write WE Fest Tickets, Box 625, Detroit Lakes 56501 or call 218–847–1340).

A nearby alternative to the festivities at Soo Pass is a lovely 43,000-acre wilderness area 18 miles northeast of Detroit Lakes that's teeming with wildlife. The rolling wooded terrain and numerous lakes and marshes of ◆ **Tamarac National Wildlife Refuge** are popular with anglers, hikers, birders, and those looking for a pleasant drive through a fine stretch of northern Minnesota landscape. The refuge headquarters, at the junction of County Highways 26 and 29, features a beautiful new interpretive center with an excellent multimedia presentation on the history and wildlife of Tamarac. Wilderness-oriented films are shown on summer weekend afternoons; for titles and show times, call (218) 847–2641.

There's a self-guided auto tour of the refuge that starts and ends at the headquarters, too. The drive follows winding gravel roads past duck wetlands, stands of wild rice, and peat bogs that support clusters of tamarac—Minnesota's only "evergreen" that drops its needles each fall. You may even see a pair of trumpeter swans that have recently reclaimed the refuge as a summer home. In winter the swans will be gone, but the refuge's 8 miles of cross-country ski trails offer their own special appeal.

POLK COUNTY

The regular customers of ◆ **Joe DiMaggio's** bar and pizza joint in Erskine will tell you that they don't care much for big-city life. One says he last traveled to St. Paul in 1965 and hasn't been drawn back since. Another claims he even avoids cities the size of Moorhead as much as possible. But clearly both of them and many of their fellow citizens are very much at home in a tavern that radiates as much New York City nostalgia— most of which has to do with the mighty Yankees—as a Coney Island hot-dog stand.

Dozens of historic photographs of the likes of Babe Ruth, Lou Gehrig, and, of course, Joe DiMaggio himself are scattered about the crowded walls. There are jerseys, hats, banners, and baseballs signed by mighty sluggers and fielders. Painted above each booth are boldface headlines lifted from the sports pages on historic occasions in Yankee Stadium. And dominating a large wall by the pool table is a delightfully rendered mural of one of the most famous moments in Yankee baseball history: Don Larson is shown unloading the final pitch of his World Series "perfect" game on October 8, 1956.

Ask Joe DiMaggio, the establishment's owner (no kidding—that's his real name), what inspired all this and he tells about his baseball-oriented boyhood in the Bronx, where he and his father (Joe Sr.) were often reminded that fate had placed them in the shadow of greatness. Mail and phone calls intended for their namesake were frequently misdirected to Joe's house. Thus in 1983, when Joe and his wife opened up a pizza place and tavern in Erskine, he decided to dedicate the place to a subject that had captured his imagination long ago. The story of how a city boy like Joe wound up in Erskine is another tale worth telling—ask him about it when you belly up to the bar.

RED LAKE COUNTY

Red Lake County is not only the smallest county in Minnesota; it also happens to be one of the flattest. And despite its size, passing through on Route 59 or some lesser road is a little like traversing the boundless waters of an ocean. There are few landmarks to gauge the passing of the miles besides an occasional stand of trees rising like an island above the distant horizon.

But when you've just about decided that this monotony will never quit, all of a sudden you stumble onto a pleasant surprise. The ◈ **Red Lake River** winds across the prairie like a beautiful wooded oasis—one that offers clear, cool flowing water and the kind of recreational opportunities that you'd expect to find only in a more woodsy environment.

The 20-mile stretch of river from St. Hilaire in Pennington County to Red Lake Falls, which flows through steep clay banks lined with hardwoods, is fine for easy canoeing and fishing, particularly for channel catfish. Then just above Red Lake Falls, the pace picks up. Three miles of nonstop rapids support Minnesota's largest commercially developed inner-tube-float-trip industry.

The first outfitter to begin full-scale operations along the banks of the Red Lake, ◈ **Voyageur's View,** claims to have hosted the world's largest inner-tubing flotilla. Some 749 persons, clinging to one another's tubes on a sunny day in 1986, made newspaper headlines as far away as Korea. This feat, however, belies the fact that most of the time tubing on the Red Lake is relatively uncrowded. Also, due to a stiff deposit required on all beverage cans, the tubing experience has managed to preserve the quality

97

of this fine natural resource. Voyageur's View also offers camping facilities. For more information write Voyageur's View, Box 48B, Red Lake Falls 56750 or call (218) 253–4329 (summer only) or 253–2031.

PENNINGTON COUNTY

If official recognition were given to the most populous creature found roaming the countryside during even the hardiest of Minnesota winters, the snowmobile might well be the uncontested recipient. In many rural communities there are sometimes more "sleds" parked on the streets and in front of taverns than cars and trucks, and Minnesota's backcountry is literally crisscrossed with snowmobile trails.

For those intrigued by the legacy of the snow machine, the Pennington County seat of Thief River Falls, where ◆**Artco Corporation** turns out the Arctic Cat snowmobile line, is likely to be an interesting summer destination, for it's during the snowless months that the following season's machines are being assembled. Visitors are welcome to stop in at the plant, located on Minnesota Highway 32 just south of town, for scheduled tours given every workday (call 218–681–8558 for times).

Hundreds of employees on the assembly line turn out an average of 130 snowmobiles per eight-hour shift. Nearby dozens of welders are at work in a row of cubicles that collectively emit more dazzling explosions of light than a fireworks show. In another room men and women are dressed in what appear to be inflated space suits to protect themselves from a cloud of dust generated as they take the rough edges off various fiberglass parts. Also, a couple of delightfully primitive-looking Arctic Cats that hark back to the snowmobile's infancy in the early 1960s are on display in the lobby.

MARSHALL COUNTY

If you're staying the night in Thief River Falls and don't mind rising at the crack of dawn, a drive to the ◆**Agassiz National Wildlife Refuge**—located on County Road 7, 18 miles northeast of town—may well result in a chance to see one of Minnesota's grandest mammals: the moose. The extensive upland and wetland areas of the 100-square-mile refuge are maintained to provide an optimal habitat for this largest member of the deer family, as well as for 280 bird species and 49 other mammals. Opportunities for observing these creatures are provided by a network of roads that wind along dikes through the extensive marshes; a booklet outlining a self-guided auto tour is available at headquarters. There is also a 100-foot observation tower that commands a magnificent view of the flat countryside in all directions. For more information call (218) 681–3720.

Thirty miles west of Agassiz, along the banks of the lazy Middle River, is one of Minnesota's most obscure state parks. ✿ **Old Mill State Park** provides an attractive setting in which to hike among the trees—a rare commodity in these parts—swim in a clear swimming hole, picnic, and camp. But perhaps its greatest attraction is a historic steam-powered gristmill that is still operational.

The simple, small wooden structure near the banks of the river next to a log-settler's cabin is actually the last of nearly a half-dozen mills built near this site by the Larson family. The first of these was a water-powered mill constructed in 1886. This building was destroyed in a flood a couple of years later and replaced by a wind-powered mill. When that didn't prove very effective, the Larsons went back to water power, moving the mill a couple times to new locations, and then finally they converted to steam about 1896.

The steam engine is fired up several times each summer on special occasions to demonstrate the milling process. The large machine, which looks a little like a railroad engine, is surprisingly quiet as it turns the 2,700-pound French burrstones, which were hauled to the site by ox cart. For more information about grinding demonstrations, write Old Mill State Park, Route 1, Box 42, Argyle 56713 or call (218) 437–8174 or, toll-free from within Minnesota, (800) 652–9747 and ask for Department of Natural Resources.

HEADWATERS

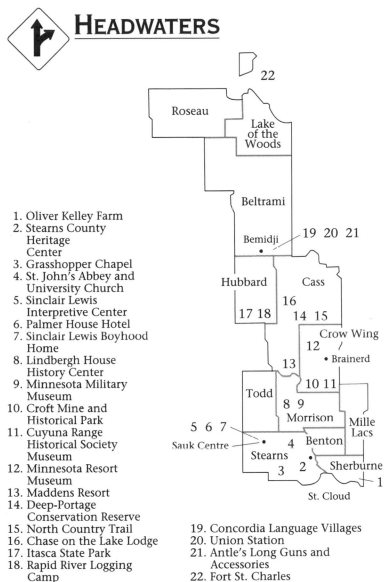

1. Oliver Kelley Farm
2. Stearns County Heritage Center
3. Grasshopper Chapel
4. St. John's Abbey and University Church
5. Sinclair Lewis Interpretive Center
6. Palmer House Hotel
7. Sinclair Lewis Boyhood Home
8. Lindbergh House History Center
9. Minnesota Military Museum
10. Croft Mine and Historical Park
11. Cuyuna Range Historical Society Museum
12. Minnesota Resort Museum
13. Maddens Resort
14. Deep-Portage Conservation Reserve
15. North Country Trail
16. Chase on the Lake Lodge
17. Itasca State Park
18. Rapid River Logging Camp
19. Concordia Language Villages
20. Union Station
21. Antle's Long Guns and Accessories
22. Fort St. Charles

Roseau
Lake of the Woods
Beltrami
Bemidji
Hubbard
Cass
Crow Wing
Brainerd
Todd
Morrison
Mille Lacs
Sauk Centre
Benton
Stearns
Sherburne
St. Cloud

Headwaters

Sherburne County

When Minnesota was organized into a territory in 1849, most of the 6,000 settlers who lived within it practiced a kind of subsistence farming. Following an agricultural tradition nearly as old as civilization, they grew a variety of crops to feed themselves, and whatever surplus there was supported a few nonfarming villagers.

Upon this scene came a young, educated son of a Boston tailor named Oliver Hudson Kelley, who staked a claim—the ❖**Oliver Kelley Farm**—along the banks of the Mississippi River (3 miles southeast of Elk River along Route 10). What he lacked in experience as a farmer Kelley made up for by reading everything he could find about the new technology and crops just becoming available. He was a natural organizer and began to propagate information on "modern" farming through numerous newspaper articles and letters. His organizational efforts culminated in the founding of the Order of the Patrons of Husbandry—or, more commonly, the Grange—a national fraternal organization of farmers whose purpose was to advance the practice of agriculture and to promote the interests of farmers.

A visit to the Kelley Farm, which is now managed by the Minnesota Historical Society, is a step back in time to this turbulent period in American agriculture when subsistence farming began to give way to the raising of large single crops for shipment to fast-growing urban centers. Kelley's organization had a spectacular if brief popularity. The intentions of the Grange struck a chord with farmers across the land—more than a million of them quickly became members—but when their most pressing economic concerns weren't effectively addressed, membership dropped off sharply.

Exhibits and multimedia presentations at a modern interpretive center chronicle this populist agriculture movement, while costumed interpretive staff at Kelley's historic farm and farmhouse bring to life the farming practices of the time. Visitors can help feed animals and sample foods prepared on the cook stove in the kitchen. Outside, men wearing wool pants even on the hottest summer days demonstrate horse-powered plowing, planting, and

Oliver Kelley Farm

harvesting. Special events, such as a Victorian wedding day and period games at the annual Independence Day celebration, make for great educational family fun. For more information call (612) 441–6896.

STEARNS COUNTY

For a city with such an ethereal name, it's ironic that the Stearns County seat of St. Cloud has such a down-to-earth nickname: The Granite City. But make no mistake, this growing urban center of 50,000 has its feet firmly on the ground, where the quarrying and processing of the area's distinctive red, pink, and gray granite have been a primary economic activity for much of the century.

The story of St. Cloud's contribution to the granite industry is told through several creative displays at the ◆ **Stearns County Heritage Center,** one of the best county historical museums in the state. Inside the spacious, modern building is a convincing two-story replica of a 1930s quarry site that illustrates how the rock was drilled and blasted free in huge chunks weighing many tons. There are also exhibits on the area's natural history, early farming, immigration, and settlement, as well as revolving displays on other aspects of local culture. Thorough research in the museum's extensive archives combines with professional design and display techniques to result in the outstanding quality of the center's exhibits. There is also a nature center, with trails for skiing and hiking, that shares the 106-acre wooded grounds with the Heritage Center. To get there, go 3 blocks south of Division Street to 235 South Thirty-third Avenue. For more information on programs and hours (the museum is open most days of the week, year-round, for a small fee), call (612) 253–8424.

If a romantic dinner for two or a fun outing with friends is what you're up to, head to **D. B. Searle's** at 18 Fifth Avenue South in downtown St. Cloud. This tall, narrow Victorian Eastlake building, which is named for a nineteenth-century St. Cloud lawyer and judge who happened to have witnessed the shooting of President Lincoln, has been transformed into a well-designed bistro that serves delicious food and oozes charm and good taste. The top floor, reserved "for lovers only" (call for reservations *at least* three months in advance), is actually a labyrinthine loft with interconnected platforms supporting a network of private booths. The third floor has a more traditional layout, accentuated by the omnipresent tones of the building's handsome woodwork. There is more dining space on the second floor, and a wonderful tavern on the ground floor is watched over by a life-size statue of a bear. The moderately priced menu features sandwiches, good steaks, and Cajun-style seafood and poultry dishes. For reservations call (612) 253–0655.

One of the most devastating natural disasters that confronted the early settlers of the Minnesota prairie was the periodic invasion of huge clouds of crop-destroying locusts. In response to a second consecutive year of this "grasshopper plague," in 1877 German Catholic farmers near the town of Cold Spring sought respite from their troubles by pledging to construct a chapel in honor of the Assumption of the Blessed Virgin. They made the vow, and as history has it, the grasshoppers disappeared the next day.

The wood-frame, Gothic Revival–style Locust Chapel built that very year survived until 1894, when it was destroyed by another violent prairie phenomenon: a tornado. In 1951 the Assumption Chapel—or, as it's commonly known, the ❖ **Grasshopper Chapel**—was reconstructed on the original site at the top of a lovely secluded knoll surrounded by oaks on Pilgrimage Road, just south of Minnesota 23 in Cold Spring, about 20 miles southwest of St. Cloud. The new chapel is built of locally quarried granite left rough on the buttressed exterior and polished to a glistening sheen inside, where a statue of the Virgin and Christ child is the only remaining article from the original building. Over the entrance is a plaque depicting the Virgin Mary ascending into heaven on a cloud, with two grasshoppers below. The chapel is open for visitation spring through fall.

There is another sacred site in the St. Cloud area that is as grand and imposing as the Grasshopper Chapel is intimate and secluded. The famous bell banner above the entrance of ❖ **St. John's Abbey and University Church** can be seen for miles protruding above the wooded slope upon which the church stands. This architectural marvel has attracted such acclaim that for the first ten years following its completion in 1961 it received more visitors than the state capitol did.

From among proposals by fifteen of the world's greatest architects, including Frank Lloyd Wright, the monks of the Benedictine Abbey selected a design for their church by Marcel Breuer, an Orthodox Jew. Breuer's concept of an unadorned, pillar-free sanctuary with walls of exposed poured concrete reflects the simplicity with which the monks carry on their lives. The prominence of the altar, near the center of the sanctuary beneath a cloudlike canopy, is a natural focal point. Illumination comes primarily from the north wall, where, behind a fantastic cantilevered, self-supported balcony, the largest stained-glass window in the world radiates magnificently. This abstract, honeycombed design was created by a member of the St. John's University art faculty, Branislaw Bak. His intent was to represent the seasons of the liturgical year—Advent, Christmas, Lent, Easter, and the Ordinary Time—through different vertical bands of color and subtly varied patterns of glass. Unifying this panorama is a series of roughly concentric circles, representing God, which draws the eye to the top and center of the window.

Outside, the bell banner stands as a monumental piece of modern poured-cement sculpture, 112 feet above ground and 100 feet across at the top, that is supported by four gracefully sweeping legs. High up in the center of this 2,500-ton creation are a large white oak cross and five bells that ring on the quarter-hour.

You're welcome to drop in and visit the church anytime and to worship with the monks if you so desire. Inside the front entrance by the beautiful granite baptismal font, you can pick up a brochure for a self-guided tour. After touring the church, you may also walk the pathways of the surrounding 2,400-acre wooded grounds, which have been designated as a wildlife sanctuary (no pets or fires are allowed). Finding St. John's church is easy: Just take the Collegeville exit off Interstate 94 and look for the bell banner to the south.

Sauk Centre has had a love-hate relationship with its most famous citizen ever since 1920, when Sinclair Lewis put the town on the world map with the publishing of his American masterpiece, *Main Street*. The first reaction to the book's less-than-flattering portrayal of life in "Gopher Prairie" was outrage—apparently many citizens thought they could see themselves in Lewis's scathing critique of small-town middle-class life. But *Main Street* and its author, who in 1930 received America's first Nobel Prize in literature, gave Sauk Centre a certain notoriety, the value of which has not escaped the notice of at least some in this otherwise undistinctive dairy town of 7,000. Today signs on Interstate 94 point the way to the Sinclair Lewis Interpretive Center, and what was once the intersection of Third Avenue and Main Street—a crossing governed by Sauk Centre's only stoplight—is now the junction of The Original Main Street and Sinclair Lewis Avenue. Even the athletes at Sauk Centre Senior High, who compete as the Mainstreeters, honor the town's literary heritage.

Four sites in Sauk Centre relate to the life and work of its best-known native son. At a rest area near the freeway you can find the ◆ **Sinclair Lewis Interpretive Center,** which also serves as a local history museum and the Chamber of Commerce. The small exhibit area features samples of Lewis's writing in various stages of the publishing process, as well as first editions of his published works and historic photographs of the town and its founders. There is also a short videotape on Lewis's life.

Sauk Centre's celebrated main intersection is dominated by the ❖ **Palmer House Hotel,** which has been restored to surpass its former state of modest elegance with the recent addition of private baths in each of the twenty-two rooms, including several Jacuzzi-equipped suites. The appeal of the place is enhanced by the fact that Sinclair Lewis worked here as a night clerk while he was in high school, though the malcontent lad was fired for daydreaming and reading on the job. Nonetheless, the hotel found its way into literary history as the "Minniemashie House" in *Main Street* and as the "American House" in *Work of Art.*

Local legend has it that when it was built in 1901, the Palmer House was the first Minnesota hotel outside the Twin Cities to offer its guests hot and cold running water and electricity in every room. The traveling salesmen who frequented the hotel during its early years were reportedly so impressed with these novelties that they wore out the light switches in six months by playing with them so incessantly. The tin ceiling and chairs in the lobby, the furniture in many of the guest rooms, the wainscoting, and the stained glass in the arched first-floor windows fared better and have survived until today. The Palmer House charges modest to expensive rates. For reservations write the Palmer House Hotel, 500 Sinclair Lewis Avenue, Sauk Centre 56378 or call (612) 352–3431.

A pilgrimage to Sauk Centre would be incomplete without a visit to the ❖ **Sinclair Lewis Boyhood Home,** located 3 blocks west of the Palmer House on Sinclair Lewis Avenue. This simple Eastlake cottage has been restored and appointed with period furnishings, earning a spot on the National Register of Historic Places. Some of the household items on display actually belonged to the Lewis family, including a junior-sized bed that was occupied by Sinclair, who was often sick during his youth. The house is open for tours daily Memorial Day through Labor Day and by arrangement the rest of the year; write the Sauk Centre Chamber of Commerce, Box 222-B, Sauk Centre 56378 or call (612) 352–5201.

MORRISON COUNTY

In one of Charles A. Lindbergh's fond memories from his boyhood summers on a farm near Little Falls, he's lying on his back

107

in tall grass, gazing for hours up at the sky. Oblivious to everything happening around him on earth, he marvels at the passing cumulus clouds, imagining what it would be like to soar among them, birdlike, in an airplane. His early dreaming about flight was nourished in a family whose members had for generations excelled at everything they undertook. Lindbergh's father was a successful lawyer and congressional representative, and his grandfather had been a prominent member of the Swedish Parliament before immigrating to the Minnesota frontier in 1860. Lindbergh, following his own path to greatness, at age twenty-five climbed aboard the single-engine *Spirit of St. Louis* on an overcast day in May 1927 and in thirty-three-and-a-half hours completed the first nonstop solo flight from New York to Paris. To his own surprise Lindy became an international hero overnight.

Still, as you'll learn for yourself upon visiting the ✤ **Lindbergh House History Center,** the crossing of the Atlantic was only one of many accomplishments in the lifetime of this remarkable person. Exhibits at the modern interpretive center, which is situated on the wooded banks of the Mississippi River, embrace the full range of Lindbergh's various achievements and interests. Parts of his first airplane, a World War I–vintage Jenny, are on display, as is a device Lindbergh helped design that is used to keep animal organs alive outside the body for the purposes of medical research. Lindy's political activities—initially he was a vocal opponent to the United States entering World War II, just as his father had argued against America's involvement in the Great War—and his later concern with ecology are also well documented. The center houses a library of films on Lindbergh, his family, and the history of human flight and offers an attractive theater for viewing them. Admission to the center, located on Minnesota 238 just south of town, is free. It is open daily from May through Labor Day and on weekends the rest of the year. Tours of the nearby Lindbergh boyhood home are also offered. For more information call (612) 632–3154.

You'll find the entrance to **Charles A. Lindbergh State Park,** named for the aviation hero's father, immediately across the street from the history center. Charles Jr., before he died in 1974, praised the establishment of this park as symbolic of civilization's greatest advancement: the valuing of life itself over the achievements of science and technology, such as the satellites now visible in the nighttime sky overhead.

Not far upstream of the Lindbergh home is an excellent museum dedicated to the Minnesota military experience. Located on the historic grounds of 53,000-acre Camp Ripley—the largest National Guard training site in the country—the ✦Minnesota Military Museum features professionally developed exhibits, including a series of displays illustrating the role Minnesota soldiers have played in every war since statehood in 1858. Another display area concerns Minnesota frontier forts, of which the original Old Fort Ripley was one. Elsewhere in the building are an exhibit on the development of small arms and a collection of war souvenirs brought home by Minnesotans from overseas. Among the latter are a handkerchief and napkin monogrammed *AH*—authenticated, says the label, as having once belonged to Adolf Hitler. The museum, located 7 miles north of Little Falls on Minnesota 115, is open free of charge Wednesday through Sunday from Memorial Day through Labor Day. Call (612) 632–7374, extension 374, for more information.

CROW WING COUNTY

The Cuyuna Iron Range is sometimes called Minnesota's forgotten iron range. Smaller than the larger ranges to the north, late to be discovered, and early to be abandoned, the Cuyuna for seventy years was nevertheless a significant producer of iron ore and, during World War II, manganese. To commemorate the history of mining on the Cuyuna, two sites in Crosby are open to the public, both of them found by following signs along Minnesota 6 in the heart of town. The ✦Croft Mine and Historical Park will take visitors on a simulated tour of the type of underground mine that was common in the area until the 1940s (for more information call 218–546–5625).

At the ✦Cuyuna Range Historical Society Museum, housed in Crosby's old train depot, a collection of mining artifacts and photographs is augmented by other local-history displays. The museum has photographs and memorabilia related to Cuyler Adams, who discovered iron on the range and named the area by combining his own name with that of his dog, Una. Also of interest are newspaper accounts and photographs of the famous 1924 Crosby mine disaster, in which forty-one miners died when their underground mine suddenly became inundated with water through an underground passage from a nearby lake. The museum is open Monday through Saturday in summer. For more information call (218) 546–5625.

Most of the historic industries that come to mind in association with the woods and lakes of northern Minnesota—trading for furs, logging the huge red and white pines, commercial fishing, mining—have come and gone relatively quickly. But in the background there has persisted a humble economic pursuit that is as long-lived as it is pervasive today: the ma-and-pa resort. And along the shore of Whitefish Lake, east of Pine River, one such establishment has dedicated a museum to this modest Minnesota institution.

The ✦ **Minnesota Resort Museum** grew out of the historical interests of the Leagjeld family, who have owned the Driftwood Resort since 1958. Eventually their collection of artifacts and photographs warranted construction of the exhibit hall that today re-creates aspects of resort life through the decades. Featured are a well-equipped, woodstove-fired kitchen and pantry, a shop area, an icehouse, a laundry, an office, and all the fixings for a traditional "shore lunch." To find the museum, go east of Pine River about 5 miles into Crow Wing County on County Road 1; then turn south on County Road 15 for 3 miles and look for signs for the Driftwood Resort. The museum is open daily in summer for a modest admission charge. For more information call (218) 568–4221.

CASS COUNTY

If you're heading north through Brainerd and need a break from the sometimes heavy traffic or if you're searching for something a bit more restful and refined than the sort of action found at Brainerd's International Raceway and the Paul Bunyan Amusement Center, you may want to stop by ✦ **Maddens Resort** on Gull Lake for a game of croquet. Now this is not exactly the kind of backyard "guerilla croquet" that you may have played as a kid. Many players on the close-cropped bent-grass courts at Maddens will be dressed all in white. The hefty wooden mallets that they swing with strategic precision cost upward of $250. They may even be drinking champagne while engaging in convivial patter between shots. This is croquet in the grand tradition of the sport, and Maddens is one of two such places in the state where the public is welcome to join in the fun.

Guest lawn fees, including equipment rental, at Maddens are moderate, and free clinics are offered several times each week. Stop by in mid-June and you can see some of the nation's best players compete in the Madden Invitational and Minnesota Championship tournaments. Maddens is located 12 miles northwest of Brainerd on County Road 77. For further information call (218) 829–2811 or, toll-free from within Minnesota, (800) 642–5363.

The 6,100-acre ◆ **Deep-Portage Conservation Reserve,** located about 10 miles east of Hackensack on County Road 46, is a beautiful natural haven offering recreational and educational activities for individuals, families, and groups. There are 40 kilometers (25 miles) of trails wandering over a hilly wooded terrain shaped by the action of two ice-age glaciers. The trails are equally divided for use between skiers and snowmobilers in the winter and are available for hiking the rest of the year. Naturalists operating out of the attractive interpretive center offer weekday and weekend programs using the surrounding lakes and forests as a classroom. For directions and information about special events, call (218) 682–2325.

Hikers may also want to explore a recently opened section of the ◆ **North Country Trail,** which, when completed, will provide a continuous footpath from New Hampshire to North Dakota. A 68-mile stretch of the trail now runs east and west through Chippewa National Forest between Remer and Walker. It may be accessed from Minnesota 371 about 5 miles north of Hackensack or from a Chippewa National Forest road near Longville. Contact the forest supervisor of the Chippewa National Forest at Walker 56484 (218–547–1044) for maps and further information.

According to a yellowing copy of the June 1921 Walker *Pilot,* at a time when the Cass County sheriff was kept busy tracking down nobodies like Frank Hillegoss and his housekeeper, Mrs. Mennypenny, for their "unholy" backyard moonshining activities in the Walker area, a grand new hotel opened its door for the first time on the shores of Leech Lake. The sixty-two-room, English Tudor–style Hotel Chase, as it was originally called, was heralded as "one of the most exquisitely designed hostelries" in the region.

The historic building still stands today under the name ✦**Chase on the Lake Lodge** and offers lakeside dining and modestly appointed bed-and-breakfast accommodations at moderate prices. There is also nightly dancing to live music (request a room far away from the lounge if you're a light sleeper). For reservations or more information, write Chase on the Lake Lodge, Box 206, Walker 56484 or call (218) 547–1531.

One weekend each winter the employees at Chase on the Lake, along with everyone else in Walker, get especially excited about an event that revolves around what is commonly regarded as one of the ugliest fish in the world. The Eelpout Festival, held every February, brings thousands of anglers to the frozen reaches of Leech Lake to try for cash prizes awarded to those able to "bag a burbot." For their part the restaurant staff at Chase on the Lake don tuxedos and long dresses and serve a formal brunch in the thick of the celebration—that is, right out there on the ice. Information on the Eelpout Festival can be obtained by calling the Leech Lake Area Chamber of Commerce at (218) 547–1313.

HUBBARD COUNTY

The headwaters of the Mississippi River are a destination of such international renown that the point could be made that they don't belong in a guidebook dedicated to undiscovered—or at least untrammeled—places. ✦**Itasca State Park,** however, in which the Father of Waters begins its epic southern journey by flowing northward at a mere trickle, has within it a number of genuinely obscure attractions that most people discover only by stumbling upon them.

Perhaps more than any other of Minnesota's sixty-four state parks, Itasca, the oldest in the state, has the feeling of a national park. The massive hand-hewn-log and stone construction of the Forest Inn Interpretive Center and the Douglas Lodge (Itasca is the only Minnesota state park to offer meals and accommodations) are reminiscent of Yosemite or Yellowstone. The scale of these buildings reflects the size of the trees to be found in the surrounding forests, too. In fact Itasca boasts the largest white and red pines on record in the state.

Both of these trees are found at marked locations along Wilderness Drive, a one-way road that winds through the northwestern quarter of the park. Having survived the past 300 years, including the onslaughts of loggers near the turn of the century, the giant white today looms 112 feet high, protruding above the surrounding forest canopy. Its trunk is massive—55 inches in diameter—and its limbs somewhat diminished, suggesting that this tree has spent most of its energy growing up, not out. Nearby, the big red, or Norway, pine tops out at 120 feet above ground. The bark of its 300-year-old trunk has a scaly, reptilelike appearance, and visible at its base are fire scars from six different blazes. Far overhead, a tangle of branches twists out in all directions like a frozen burst from a fireworks display.

The short path leading to the big red pine also passes by one of the state's more interesting archaeological landmarks. A plaque along the banks of a small creek marks a bison kill site where 8,000 years ago a group of prehistoric hunters slaughtered sixteen giant bison en masse, perhaps by driving them off a now-nonexistent cliff.

For more information about lodging, meals, recreational opportunities, and the extensive naturalist programs offered at Itasca, write the park manager at Itasca State Park, Lake Itasca 56460 or call (218) 266–3654 or, toll-free from within Minnesota, (800) 652–9747 and ask for DNR.

One tourist-oriented destination near Park Rapids provides visitors with insights into the era that saw the transformation of Minnesota's woodlands from magnificent pine climax forests into a mixed bag of second-growth species such as aspen, birch, spruce, and balsam fir. The ◈ **Rapid River Logging Camp,** located 5 miles north of town on County Road 18, features several logging exhibits and an all-you-can-eat lumberjack cook shanty—the camp's main attraction—that provides three inexpensive meals daily, Memorial Day through Labor Day. For more information about the camp, call (218) 732–3444.

Beltrami County

Though they're miles from the United Nations, one day each summer Bemidji's ◈ **Concordia Language Villages** explode in a polylingual, multicultural celebration of world unity that casts a shadow all the way to the UN Plaza. For one day in July or August, hundreds of young people participating in the nine

113

Concordia Language Villages programs throughout Minnesota converge on Bemidji for an international festival.

Participants in the acclaimed Concordia College–sponsored program live in Russian, Finnish, Chinese, Norwegian, French, Swedish, Danish, German, Japanese, or Spanish "villages," in which their American belongings have been surrendered upon arrival at "customs." Students exchange their familiar language, their currency, and even their own names for those derived from their new culture.

Guests of the festival (it is open to the public free of charge) can participate in this experience as the young people emerge from their adopted cultures to share ethnic foods, crafts, music, and gifts. Professional folk dancers and musicians add to the entertainment. Festival revelers also have an opportunity to see the traditional German and Norwegian architecture of the Bemidji Language Villages sites. For more information call toll-free within Minnesota (800) 247–1044; outside Minnesota (800) 222–4750.

As you're passing through downtown Bemidji, you're bound to catch sight of one of Minnesota's classic pieces of oversized civic roadside "art." Paul Bunyan and Babe the Blue Ox stand so stiffly at attention at the intersection of Third Street and Bemidji Avenue that your limbs ache just looking at them. This structure, built in 1937, is one of the most photographed statues in the United States—or at least that's what they'll tell you at the Chamber of Commerce next door.

Before leaving town you may want to stop for a bite to eat at ◆ **Union Station,** a restaurant and bar in the historic depot building at First Street and Beltrami Avenue. Employing much tasteful woodwork and featuring a dramatic railroad mural of grand proportions in the main dining room, Union Station serves good, moderately priced Italian and American food. Champagne brunch is offered on Sundays. For reservations call (218) 751–9261.

One doesn't have to attend too many of the Gopher State's historic festivals before encountering a peculiar species of Minnesotan. He is dressed from head to toe in buckskin and furs; he assumes a historically derived manner that can, with generosity, best be described as uncouth; and he dotes on his bowie knife and black-powder musket.

Those taken by the presence of this character—or perhaps just curious about his origins—may want to pay a visit to an obscure shop called ❖**Antle's Long Guns and Accessories,** located on Route 2 just west of Bemidji. The approach to this humble establishment follows a bumpy gravel road through a wooded graveyard of decomposing automobiles. Displayed inside is a varied assortment of muskets, beads and other clothing accessories, muzzle-cleaning supplies, and gunpowder, as well as a selection of books on how to become an authentic black-powder buff. Roy Antle is available to instruct the unenlightened regarding the safe use of his muskets on the shooting range out back.

As its owner is a member in good standing of the Bemidji Hangfires Black Powder Club, Roy's shop is also a good source of information on the northland's largest Black Powder Rendezvous, held each June somewhere near Bemidji. Those attending can look forward to "paper punchin', primitive shooting, gun trading, and knife and spear throwing" among other activities, only some of which are claimed to be suitable for kids and women. For more information call Antle's at (218) 751–4752.

LAKE OF THE WOODS COUNTY

When French explorer Pierre La Verendrye built ❖**Fort St. Charles** in 1732 on an island in what is now called Lake of the Woods, it was the most northwesterly settlement of Europeans in North America. For ten years the fort was an important fur trading post for La Verendrye and his sons, who used it as a base of operations for their explorations of the Canadian Northwest. The fort also became the burial place of a French Jesuit priest, Father Jean Aulneau, and nineteen of his companions, who were killed on another island by a Dakota war party in 1736.

Visitors can reach the fort by boat from Warroad or Baudette (about a 50-mile ride) or by car from Warroad, 63 miles (the final 23 of which are gravel) through a section of Manitoba to Minnesota's Northwest Angle, where a number of resorts can provide easy boat access to Magnusson Island. A reconstructed palisade and log chapel stand today on the site of the original fort, and markers show where other buildings once stood. For a brochure with more information on the fort, write R. M. Tegeder, 5867 West 139th Street, Apple Valley 55124.

ARROWHEAD

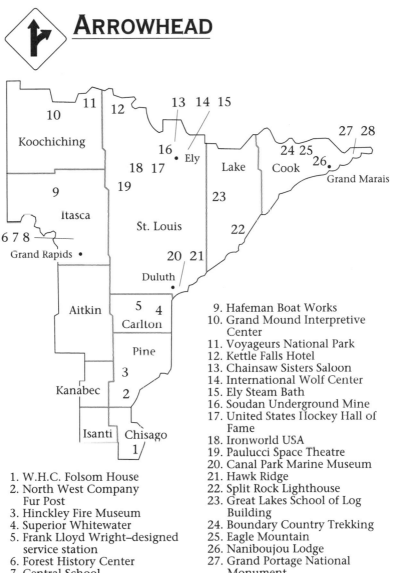

10 Koochiching
11
12
13 14 15
16 • Ely
18 17
Lake
24 25
26 •
Cook
27 28
Grand Marais

9
Itasca
19

6 7 8
Grand Rapids •

St. Louis
23
22

20 21
Duluth •

Aitkin
5 4
Carlton

Pine
3

Kanabec
2

Isanti
Chisago
1

1. W.H.C. Folsom House
2. North West Company
Fur Post
3. Hinckley Fire Museum
4. Superior Whitewater
5. Frank Lloyd Wright–designed
service station
6. Forest History Center
7. Central School
8. Hill Annex Mine

9. Hafeman Boat Works
10. Grand Mound Interpretive
Center
11. Voyageurs National Park
12. Kettle Falls Hotel
13. Chainsaw Sisters Saloon
14. International Wolf Center
15. Ely Steam Bath
16. Soudan Underground Mine
17. United States Hockey Hall of
Fame
18. Ironworld USA
19. Paulucci Space Theatre
20. Canal Park Marine Museum
21. Hawk Ridge
22. Split Rock Lighthouse
23. Great Lakes School of Log
Building
24. Boundary Country Trekking
25. Eagle Mountain
26. Naniboujou Lodge
27. Grand Portage National
Monument
28. Grand Portage State Park

ARROWHEAD

CHISAGO COUNTY

Minnesota's logging boom came early to the St. Croix River valley. The grand bluffs and the valleys of the St. Croix's tributaries, thick with giant white and red pine, were the first areas in the state to suffer the effects of the sawyer's blade. By the mid-1850s, with each spring runoff the river became a highway of logs, each stamped with the distinctive mark of the company whose workers had felled it, all bound for the sawmills of Stillwater.

When these huge log booms reached Taylors Falls, however, they often ran into trouble. The river here enters the St. Croix Dalles, a constricted, steep-walled basalt canyon with a sharp ninety-degree bend at its center. The Dalles was the site of some truly spectacular logjams (check out the pictures on the walls of Taylors Falls's Chisago House restaurant) that kept river workers busy for weeks as they sought to keep the logs moving by whatever means was necessary—including, at times, large charges of dynamite.

In an accommodating gesture to the boisterous loggers who frequented Taylors Falls each spring, the community erected a jail as one of the early public buildings. Built in 1856, this stone structure afforded an easy escape to anyone sober enough to climb over the top of the cell wall. The fact that it apparently served its function for twenty-nine years may be a testament to the sorry state of its occupants, but for whatever reason, in 1885 the town finally decided to invest $311 in the construction of a newer and more secure facility. It is this building, the **Historic Taylors Falls Jail,** that now houses a more genteel breed of inmate as one of the state's most unusual bed-and-breakfast establishments.

Julie and Al Kunz, who keep an eye on the lockup from their home next door, have tastefully restored the building in keeping with its original two-by-four cribbing construction, in which the exterior walls were formed by securing the boards sandwich-style on top of one another. The building rents for moderate to expensive rates (guests cook their own breakfasts) and, with the sofa bed in the living area, can sleep four. Write the Kunzes at 102 Government Road, Taylors Falls 55084 or call (612) 465–3112 for reservations.

If you can swing a pass from the warden, you'll find plenty of engaging distractions in and around Taylors Falls. Just a block away from the jail is the entrance to **Interstate State Park,** where there are hiking trails through the Dalles, with its fantastic water-sculpted rock formations. Rock climbers from the Twin Cities frequent this area, as do kayakers who come to frolic in the rapids just downstream of the Route 8 highway bridge. An excursion boat offers rides downstream in summer, and the park has a canoe-rental facility as well.

To get a feel for the world inhabited by the town's early residents, you can tour the historic ◆**W.H.C. Folsom House,** located just a block up Government Road from the jail. This 1855 Greek Revival home of a local logger, general-store owner, and state politician is the most significant building in the town's Angel Hill District, which has been listed in its entirety on the National Register of Historic Places. Almost all the furnishings in the house are original. The half-hour guided tour reveals many day-to-day details of the family's life while at the same time providing a glimpse into a particular point in history. The family was touched by the Civil War, as is evidenced by the blue-and-gray uniform on display that was worn by William Folsom's son, Wyman. A local newspaper on a desk in the library interprets the significance of the assassination of President Lincoln. Tours are given daily, for a modest fee, from Memorial Day to mid-October; for more information call (612) 465–3125.

PINE COUNTY

As the first Europeans began making their way west to the land that was to become Minnesota, they arrived via a mode of travel that was true to the old adage "When in Rome, do as the Romans do." The birchbark canoes of Indian design that these explorers used proved so well suited to the watery landscape that the canoe remained essential to the region's first commercial enterprise— the fur trade. Thus, the banks of a river like the Snake would have been the perfect place for an operation like the ◆**North West Company Fur Post,** which today stands in all its early nineteenth-century splendor north of Country Road 7, about 2 miles west of Pine City.

This living history site, managed by the Minnesota Historical Society, offers you an intriguing immersion into one of the state's most romantic eras. The French Canadian voyageurs whom you will find living inside the exactingly re-created rough log palisade were a notoriously colorful and lusty bunch. Paddling heavily ladened canoes and portaging loads of 180 pounds and up from dawn to dusk throughout summer, the voyageurs were so high-spirited that they reputedly could not be kept from singing. In their boisterous way they will teach you how to throw a tomahawk and start a fire using flint and steel, while spinning tales about how they spent their time at the post (which was occupied in the winter of 1804–1805) trading guns, blankets, beads, and metal cookware with trappers belonging to local Ojibway bands.

The North West Company Fur Post—which is open free of charge Tuesday through Saturday, May through early September—also gives you a glimpse into the incredibly vast scale of this Canadian-controlled fur trade empire. When the men at the post paddled to Grand Portage (see the description under Cook County, page 156) in early summer for their company's annual rendezvous, they were joined by compatriots from as far away as Montreal and the arctic tundra of the Canadian Northwest. For more information call (612) 629–6356.

Perhaps the most tragic legacy of Minnesota's turn-of-the-century logging boom was the devastating fire that completely consumed Hinckley and five other towns nearby in the hot, dry summer of 1894. The ◆ **Hinckley Fire Museum**—located in the town's defunct train depot at 106 Old Highway 61 and open daily for a small fee, May through October—has been dedicated to this singularly destructive event. Because of an accumulated effect of years of clear-cut logging, in which a thick mantle of limbs from the felled giant pines was left like tinder on the ground, there had been a number of small fires ignited through the summer, many by sparks from passing steam locomotives. Finally, on September 1 conditions were at their driest and a strong wind fanned one of these blazes into a fire storm that swept across 320,000 acres of land, destroying everything in its path. The museum's multimedia presentation, photographs, mural, and static displays of melted household artifacts recount the fate of the 418 persons killed in the conflagration, as well as those few who escaped by fleeing to nearby rivers and ponds.

CARLTON COUNTY

Ask a knowledgeable Minnesotan to steer you toward the Grand Portage and you're likely to find yourself cruising along Lake Superior's resplendent north shore, headed for the Canadian border. However, the 9-mile climb from the shores of Gitche Gumee up and over the Sawtooth Mountains that was made famous by the voyageurs (see the section on Cook County) isn't the only grand portage in the state. The spectacular cataracts of the St. Louis River in its final descent before entering a placid estuary that leads to Duluth harbor also precipitated a major carrying place for early explorers and fur traders seeking passage from the Great Lakes to the Mississippi watershed. This rugged valley, too, was known as the Grand Portage.

Today the area surrounding the St. Louis River Dalles is preserved as **Jay Cooke State Park,** which offers great hiking and skiing trails, camping, and picnicking along the banks of the river. But if you haven't the time or inclination to explore the area under your own locomotion, there's much to be gained by a drive along Minnesota Highway 210 between Interstate 35 and Minnesota 23, which parallels the river on the north side. The road winds up and over the rugged contours of the valley for 9 miles and could almost fool you into thinking you've been detoured onto an Appalachian highway.

If, however, hiking isn't quite adventuresome enough for your tastes, stop by ◆**Superior Whitewater,** just 1 or 2 miles east of Carlton on Highway 210. Spring through fall, Superior Whitewater conducts professionally guided whitewater-rafting trips down an undeveloped stretch of the St. Louis just upstream of Jay Cooke State Park. The rafts accommodate six paddle-wielding passengers, each outfitted with a life jacket and instructed by experienced guides in the skills required to pilot the vessel; two-person inflatable kayaks are also available. The rapids on this section of the river begin gently enough and then grow in size and intensity as you progress downstream. By the time you reach Electric Ledge—a thrilling 6-foot chute formed where the water tumbles over a river-wide bedrock dike—you're ready for the exhilarating splash in the face that you're likely to get.

The excitement of Minnesota's only whitewater-rafting experience lasts about two and a half hours and is expensively priced.

You should make reservations in advance by writing Superior Whitewater, 950 Chestnut Street, Carlton 55718 or by calling (218) 384-4637.

As you cruise through Carlton's main intersection, the junction of Minnesota Highways 210 and 45, you may notice a slightly down-at-the-mouth little eating establishment on the corner called **Charlotte's Cafe**—it's the one with the sign out front that reads CAFE OPEN REAL PEOPLE This is the domain of Charlotte Zacher, who has been behind the grill since 1928 cooking what another sign inside says are THE BEST HAMBURGERS ON EARTH OR ANY OTHER PLACE. Dressed in flowing pastel evening gowns or hot pants and white go-go boots and wearing bold quantities of jewelry about her pompadoured silver-white hair, Charlotte is both a generous friend to her neighbors and regular customers (who often are surprised with birthday cakes produced in their honor) and something of a media celebrity. Her inexpensive homemade soups and burgers have been satisfying wayward travel writers, television producers (*Real People* and *PM Magazine* have both paid their respects), and locals alike—they just may do the same for you.

Before you disappear into the northern forests, a final stop in Carlton County should be made at the southeast corner of the junction of Minnesota Highways 45 and 33 in Cloquet. Here, amid gas fumes and the honking of cars, stands the world's only ◆ **Frank Lloyd Wright–designed service station.** Since 1957 this Phillips 66 franchise has been humbly serving the fossil-fuel needs of countless customers who have pulled up beneath the steep, angular, cantilevered roof, perhaps unaware that they were in the presence of architectural greatness. Thus forewarned, you won't make the same mistake.

ITASCA COUNTY

Grand Rapids, the Itasca County seat, is an attractive old logging town that hasn't quit. The looming buildings of the Blandin Paper Company, which line the banks of a not-yet-so-mighty Mississippi River in the heart of the city, stand as living testament to the days when the decimated giant pine gave way to the cutting of pulpwood. Free tours of the facility are offered regularly and follow the high-tech, step-by-step transformation of locally harvested balsam and poplar into fifteen-ton spools of glossy magazine stock that may eventually find its way into your home as *Time* or *Newsweek*. For more information on tours, call (218) 327–6228.

Back when pine was king, of course, life was a whole lot simpler, as you'll discover for yourself if you pay a visit to the Minnesota Historical Society's wonderful ◆ **Forest History Center.** You'll find this painstakingly resurrected turn-of-the-century logging camp and interpretive center a few miles west of town on County Road 70, near Golf Course Road.

The modern interpretive center houses an excellent exhibit on the history of mankind's relationship with Minnesota's forests. From now-extinct Native American cultural traditions to the most recent trends in conservation, this story is told through multimedia presentations, static displays, and photographs. A highlight is a short film of the last logging drive in Minnesota, which took place on the Little Fork River in 1937. Expert "whitewater men" can be seen hopping nimbly from log to log, while others guide huge "wanigans"—rafts supporting the crew's kitchen and bunkhouse—through the rapids.

Even though it may look like summer outside to you, it's December 15, 1900, in the Northwoods Logging Company camp, located a short hike through the woods from the interpretive center. In fact as your guide explains before you enter the first of several hand-hewn log buildings, the crew is still looking for some hardy men and women to fill a few jobs for the season. Highly entertaining and extremely knowledgeable costumed characters populating the camp provide opportunities for a little on-the-job training to help you decide if spending the winter as a "road monkey," assistant cook, or sawyer is for you. Unfortunately, as most folks quickly learn, their backwoods savvy qualifies them only for the bottom-rung position of road monkey, whose job it was to throw straw in front of log-burdened sleighs on the icy downhills and collect the "road apples" dropped in the wake of the powerful draft horses.

Besides visiting the bunkhouse, the notoriously ornery cook and her humble assistants, the earthy barn boss and blacksmith, and the solitary saw sharpener, you also get a chance to chat with a 1930s Forest Service ranger in his nearby cabin. Finally, you can visit a replica floating kitchen, or wanigan, of the type once used by logging crews as they drove their logs downstream. All facilities at the center are open daily mid-May through mid-October, and special events, such as a kids' weekend in mid-June and a woodcrafts festival in mid-July, are scheduled annually. The interpretive center is open afternoons through winter. There is a small admission fee. For more information call (218) 327–4482.

Since its construction in 1902, Grand Rapids's ❖ **Central School**—located at the intersection of Highways 2 and 169—has no doubt seen a lot of students gazing wistfully out of its Romanesque Revival arched windows. Today the attractive building has been preserved as a center for the area's historic heritage and the arts. Also, on the first floor, in what for many years was actually the first-grade room, is the First Grade, an inexpensive restaurant serving very good homemade soups, sandwiches, and pies in an atmosphere likely to rekindle some long-forgotten grade-school memories.

Even more nostalgia is in store on the building's third floor, where the Itasca County Historical Museum has dedicated considerable space to Grand Rapids's most famous citizen. Judy Garland—born Francis Gumm in 1922 to Grand Rapids movie-theater owner Frank Gumm—lived in town only until she was four. But by then she had already gotten a taste for the limelight, having delighted her father's customers by dancing on the movie-house stage at age two-and-a-half. Commemorating her career are videos of *The Wizard of Oz* and other Garland films, a yellow brick road outside the building, and a collection of photographs, albums, and what is claimed to be the nation's largest display of Garland memorabilia. (The Gumm House, not open to the public, can be seen a few blocks away at 727 Second Avenue Northeast. Also, an annual festival in honor of Judy Garland is held in Grand Rapids.) Other exhibits in the museum—which charges a modest admission fee and is open year-round most days of the week—focus on aspects of Itasca County history. Elsewhere in the building a large art gallery features works of local artists.

In Ojibway mythology there is a sleeping giant called "Mesabi," and it was believed that the huge ridge of ancient granite stretching 50 miles north and east of Grand Rapids was its home. Though they may not have been able to conceive of just how their giant was to be awakened or what it would mean to America's burgeoning twentieth-century industries, the Mesabi and the adjacent Vermilion Iron Range did indeed house a giant that for decades yielded vast quantities of the richest iron ore on earth.

In Calumet—at the western end of the Mesabi, 18 miles east of Grand Rapids on Route 169—there is a must-visit site for anyone who wants to gain a firsthand perspective on just how Minnesota's iron-ore giant was shaken to life. The ◈ **Hill Annex Mine** was in continuous operation from 1903 to 1978, when it was shut down practically overnight and sold to the state for a token fee. Run since 1988 by the Department of Natural Resources as Minnesota's sixty-fourth and newest state park, Hill Annex allows visitors to examine every aspect of the mining process—from the bottom of the pit to the top of the waste-rock piles looming more than 500 feet overhead.

The tour begins at the old Hill Annex Clubhouse, which was built in the 1930s as a gathering place for managers who lived with their families in adjacent company houses at this "location" (a worker-habitation site) near the edge of the ever-growing pit; the miners, by contrast, kept to their own kind in bunkhouses on the other side of the tracks. Well-designed exhibits and excellent larger-than-life photographs in the clubhouse chronicle changing life-styles and technologies at the mine. Upstairs are re-created location living quarters, a chemistry lab, and a foreman's office. Another room has an oral-history library and a computer-operated photograph file that are open to visitors.

This orientation complete, the visitor should get ready to board a colorful bus for a ninety-minute tour of the mine itself. Much of this time is spent exploring the processing plant, which separated ore from waste rock, and the complex network of conveyors that carried these materials to their respective destinations.

Though the Hill Annex was relatively small by comparison with other mines on the range, it is an awesome sight nonetheless. More than sixty-three million tons of ore were extracted from the 640-acre pit, whose bottom is now flooded with water. The decades of blasting and carving required to move all that rock have created a landscape that is simultaneously beautiful and discomforting to behold. Looking out from the rim, one sees the water glistening far below as if from the bottom of a spectacular desert canyon. But the place is also raw and desolate, occupied here and there by rusting hulks of machinery that look puny from afar and cumbersome and lifeless up close.

Bus tours at the Hill Annex are run on the hour, for a small fee, daily from Memorial Day through September. For information on special geology tours or for group reservations, write the Hill Annex Mine, Box 376, Calumet 55716 or call (218) 247–7215.

There are so few serious practitioners of the lost art of birchbark-canoe building in the United States that they can practically be counted on one hand. But as is only appropriate to a state whose history is so deeply indebted to the canoe, one of the nation's greatest builders can be found in the heart of Minnesota's northwoods. As you're cruising north on Minnesota 6 from Deer River, passing the settlements of Bowstring and Talmoon in a blur, the thick forests on either side of the road are suddenly interrupted by the Big Fork River and a large tar-paper shed on its banks, with a couple of graceful-looking bark vessels displayed out front. The sign above the door reads ◆ HAFEMAN BOAT WORKS.

Ray Boessel inherited this canoe-building business from his grandfather-in-law, Bill Hafeman, in 1981, and since then he has supported himself by producing up to seventeen canoes a year. The elder master learned the trade by necessity after moving to Big Fork in 1920, when the river route to town was a far-better option than the area's rudimentary roads. Although Bill's maiden voyage in his first canoe carried him to town in four hours, it took him two *days* to get home. Over the years he greatly refined the canoe-building skills that Ray, in his gentle, friendly way, is glad to share with you. You'll learn all that's involved in his ancient trade— from cutting bark from live birches when the sap is flowing in early summer to collecting the long spruce roots for lashing the canoe together to completing the final stages of assembly. You can even test-paddle one of the finished products on the river to discover how strong, pliable, and lovely these canoes truly are.

In case you want to take one of these watercraft home with you to join the ranks of such proud owners as Charles Kuralt and Lady Bird Johnson, be prepared for a four-figure price tag. For more information you can write Ray at RR 1, Box 187, Big Fork 56628 or call (218) 743–3709.

KOOCHICHING COUNTY

The Big Fork River has been a heavily traveled river throughout most of the human era. Its prominent role in the 12,000-year human history of the north country is revealed by a visit to the ❖ **Grand Mound Interpretive Center,** located at the confluence of the Big Fork and Rainy rivers on Minnesota Highway 11, 17 miles west of International Falls.

At the end of a short trail leading from the Grand Mound Interpretive Center building toward the heavily wooded banks of the Rainy, the forest canopy suddenly opens up to reveal a huge dome-shaped earthwork covered with ferns. This mysterious cultural creation that masquerades as a hillock is surrounded by four smaller ancient burial mounds. Several large trees growing on the Grand Mound's flanks only hint at how old the structure actually is. To plumb the depths of its age and to gain some idea of the mound's significance, you would do well to spend a hour or so at the interpretive center, where an excellent video and labyrinthine exhibit on northern Minnesota prehistory flesh out the story.

The Grand Mound was the largest of some 10,000 burial mounds that the first Europeans encountered upon exploring the land that was to become Minnesota. Some of these mounds resembled animal or human forms, others were linear or cone shaped, and many were located at the junctions of rivers. Apparently the Indians of the time had no explanation as to when or by whom the mounds were made. This reinforced a common belief of early scholars that the "simple savages" then living in North America were incapable of building the mounds, and there was wild speculation as to who should be credited with their creation. The bones and simple artifacts unearthed by enthusiastic investigators and curio hunters were attributed to druids, ancient Egyptians, prehistoric Chinese, and even pioneers from the lost city of Atlantis.

More recent excavations by contemporary archaeologists have produced evidence that the Grand Mound was built by a number of different prehistoric Indian cultures from 200 B.C. to A.D. 1400. Not much is known about what significance mound burials may have had for these peoples, though scientists suggest that the societies that produced the mounds were relatively complex and hierarchical (only selected, hence presumably more important, individuals were entombed) and that their members seem to have been greatly preoccupied with death.

The Grand Mound Interpretive Center is open free of charge Tuesday through Sunday, May through early September. Call (218) 279–3332 for more information.

In winter the Rainy River border town of International Falls often receives the dubious distinction of being identified as the nation's "cold spot." But when summer comes, the area around "Frostbite Falls" shows another face altogether. Eleven miles east of downtown, the magnificent 219,000-acre expanse of ✦ **Voyageurs National Park,** Minnesota's only national park, draws visitors seeking a full spectrum of waterborne recreational opportunities. So much of this relatively unknown park is covered with water—there are more than thirty lakes, five of which are quite large—that no roads lead into its interior. Thus the most common means of travel are by motorboat, houseboat, sailboat, canoe, kayak, and floatplane. Excellent hiking routes are found on the densely forested Kabetogama Peninsula in the interior, but the only access to the peninsula on the U.S. side requires the services of an air- or waterborne ferry. During the chilly winter months, Voyageurs's thick lake ice and plentiful snow invite exploration by snowmobile and on skis.

If you don't happen to have your own watercraft along on your visit to Voyageurs, don't despair. Departing at least once daily during most of the summer from the Rainy Lake Visitor Center on Black Bay, 11 miles east of International Falls on County Road 11, is the *Pride of Rainy Lake.* Many excursions on this large cruiser are narrated by Park Service naturalists who tell tales of the lively human history of the park—including exploits of Indians, voyageurs, gold miners, and lumberjacks—as they interpret aspects of the park's pristine boreal forest environment (prices for these trips are inexpensive to moderate). Excursions across Black Bay via large fur trade canoes are also offered for no charge. The historic exhibits, orientation video, and bookstore at the visitor's center are also well worth an hour of your time.

For more information about the park, write the Superintendent, Voyageurs National Park, Box 50, International Falls 56649 or call (218) 283–9821. For general information on cruises aboard the *Pride of Rainy Lake,* call Rainy Lake Cruises at (218) 286–5470;

Kettle Falls Hotel

for information about naturalist-guided trips on the same boat, call the Rainy Lake Visitors Center at (218) 286–5258.

St. Louis County

Much of Voyageurs National Park is also accessible from northwestern St. Louis County. The end of the Ash River Trail, County Road 129, is a jumping-off place for the backcountry lakes of the Kabetogama Peninsula, which is also the site of the park's most unusual civilized attraction: Minnesota's remotest and perhaps most historically colorful hotel.

The ◆ **Kettle Falls Hotel** landing (travel by boat is the only means of getting here) is quite close to the now-dammed Kettle Falls, which marks the international border and connects the Kabetogama Peninsula with Canadian soil. Following a compre-

129

hensive Park Service–funded restoration that was completed in 1988, the hotel sits proudly among the tall pines at the end of a long wooded walkway. The building is gleaming with fresh white paint, and cheerful red-and-white striped awnings adorn each window. A huge wraparound screened porch embraces the lower level and provides a pleasant site for dining, reading, or taking in the evening air. The rooms upstairs, which command a moderate price, are appointed with simple antiques and antique reproductions (all share common bathroom facilities). And then there's the bar . . .

According to its brochure the Kettle Falls was built in 1913 to provide a "stopping place" for loggers who were endeavoring to rout the surrounding forests of the ubiquitous giant red and white pines. But corner the hotel manager, and you may learn just what induced those loggers to frequent the place. He can tell you about the extensive bootlegging and smuggling operations that were run out of the hotel during Prohibition (the woods on the Canadian side of the border provided an ideal site for a still). He may mention something of the pervasive gambling that took place, and he might just hint at another enterprise that was once central to the Kettle Falls's appeal.

But if the manager leaves some gaps in the story, just find your way to the hotel bar and, with luck, the bartender will fill in the rest. This room is adorned with signed photographs of leering sirens and framed calendar girls of a bygone era—perhaps the same faces that gazed down on the lumberjacks as they waited to take their turns upstairs with some of the hotel's female employees. In their exuberance these customers danced on top of the bar until it was reduced to splinters under their hobnailed boots.

If, after hearing about all this, you find that you have a little trouble walking straight and the surroundings seem a bit out of kilter, console yourself with the knowledge that the barroom floor really does slope rather drastically toward the door. The reconstruction preserved in the warped foundation a 2-foot drop in elevation when measured from the summit of a hump near the pool table (which appears to be desperately maintaining its equilibrium) to the distant corner.

The Kettle Falls has several housekeeping cabins available, as well as boat and canoe rentals. Home-cooked meals from a limited menu are served daily in the dining room. For more information contact the Kettle Falls Hotel, Ash River Trail, Orr 55771 or call (218) 374–3511.

Renting a houseboat from **Minnesota Voyageur Houseboats** is another way to gain access to the distant bays and numerous fishing holes of the park. Equipped with every convenience a landlubber could ask for, these floating mobile homes cruise at slow speed by day and are nosed up on protected beaches at night. Depending on size of party, length of trip, and degree of luxury sought, houseboat rentals are moderately to expensively priced. Contact Minnesota Voyageur Houseboats at Ash River Trail, Orr 55771 or call (218) 374–3571.

The Echo Trail is a remote Minnesota backroad that delivers all of the pristine enchantment conjured up by its name. Flanked on both sides for most of its 60 winding, hilly miles by the famed million-acre Boundary Waters Canoe Area (BWCA) wilderness, the Echo can afford drivers glimpses of deer, moose, bear, and possibly even the elusive eastern timber wolf. As it meanders between Echo Lake, about 6 miles south of the little town of Crane Lake on County Road 24, and the north shore of Shagawa Lake near Ely, the Echo Trail skirts several lakeshores from which, on a calm summer evening, you may hear the resonant call of a loon across the water.

St. Paul YMCA Camp du Nord is one Echo Trail establishment that beckons families in search of an unusual summer vacation experience. Du Nord, located on County Road 644 (also known as the North Arm Road) about 9 miles down the Echo from its eastern terminus, is a family camp—meaning that it combines many of the features typically found at a resort with a creative variety of program activities for all ages. Upholding a strong wilderness ethic, du Nord staff lead families on canoe trips into the BWCA and offer naturalist-guided hikes and other environmentally oriented activities. Campwide cookouts and campfires develop a robust sense of community spirit, while daily activities for different age-groups provide parents and kids with opportunities to mix with their peers. Families who attend the inexpensive, week-long summer sessions (advance reservations are required) can camp out or stay in rustic housekeeping cabins, many of which are perched along the rugged shore of the north arm of Burntside Lake. For more information write Camp du Nord, 1761 University Avenue, St. Paul 55104 or call (612) 645–7919.

Does Camp du Nord sound too wholesome for your tastes? Then retrace your steps about a half-mile east along the Echo Trail from the North Arm Road to where an anonymous track disappears into the forest, this time to the north. Forest Service Road 459, as it's designated by a small sign, will give you a progressively certain sense that you're headed for oblivion, particularly after mile 3, when you turn left at the T intersection to join a ragged, two-tire track whose bumps will nearly slow you to a crawl. Then you cross a little creek on a dubious-looking wooden bridge—the kind where you pray that you car is wide enough as you blindly aim your tires so that they might be supported by the separate wooden planks beneath—and the road suddenly ends.

The simple wood-frame building in front of you with the plastic flamingos in the yard is the ◆ **Chainsaw Sisters Saloon.** Tending bar you will probably find owner Michelle Carlson, one of a pair of brawny twins who gained their genteel alias while employed by the Forest Service to keep BWCA portages clear of deadfalls (Michelle's sister and former tavern-owning partner, Marlene, has moved on to other adventures). Following a blowout land-acquisition celebration in September 1987—during which, it is rumored, one of the twins broke some guy's arm while mud wrestling—these two women literally carved their establishment out of the surrounding woods. There's no electricity at the Chainsaw Sisters, nor is there a telephone. But the beer is cold, and there's enough light given off by the gas wall lamps to inform your contemplations of a local legend concerning the two friendly women behind the bar: Did they or did they not outlast the entire all-male Ely ice-rescue squad in a contest to see who could remain submerged the longest in the ice-capped waters of Shagawa Lake?

The Chainsaw Sisters aren't likely to be the only characters you'll meet if you spend some time visiting the wilderness frontier town of Ely. The community's past and present are thick with the exploits of prospectors, lumberjacks, and miners against a backdrop of prehistoric activity that stretches back thousands of years.

To get a sense of the breadth and depth of Ely's past, you may want to pay a visit to the **Vermilion Interpretive Center** at Vermilion Community College, located at 1900 East Camp Street. Exhibits at the center capture the many ways that Ojibway Indians, French Canadian voyageurs, Swedish loggers, and Finnish miners have interacted among themselves and left their mark on the woodlands that dominate the landscape. There is also an exhibit commemorating Ely resident Will Steger, leader of a spectacularly successful self-contained international dogsled expedition to the North Pole in 1986. The interpretive center is open Wednesday through Saturday from October through April and daily in the summer. A modest admission fee is charged.

The howl of a lone wolf echoing across a lake conjures up images of the northern wilderness like nothing else. And the Minnesota legislature, which presides over a state graced with the largest population of wolves in the lower forty-eight (1994 estimates place the population at 1,800 to 2,000), has decreed that an interpretive center be built to honor the wolf and educate people about this much-abused and -misunderstood creature. Ely's ◈ **International Wolf Center,** on Route 169 just east of town, gives people the straight scoop about wolves through imaginative hands-on programs and an award-winning exhibit on the relationship of wolves to humans of all cultures.

Art, literature, interactive videos, a large diorama of a wolf pack bringing down a white-tailed deer, and other displays at the Wolf Center stimulate thinking about the many ways humans have mythologized and romanticized the wolf over the centuries and across the continents. Fables and images range from St. Francis of Assisi to Adolf Hitler, from Lon Cheny to Romulus and Remus.

Several times each day wolf handlers enter an enclosure and introduce visitors (who watch from behind plate-glass windows) to the center's resident pack. A wolf-ecology day camp for children, summer howling trips for families, and hands-on research expeditions for adults round out the offerings. The center is open for a modest fee daily, May through mid-October, and on Tuesdays and weekends the rest of the year. For more information about programs, call toll-free (800) ELY–WOLF.

Adjacent to the Wolf Center on Highway 169 stand two log buildings that commemorate the life and times of a most unusual wilderness pioneer. Every log in the **Dorothy Molter Museum** was moved by volunteers, without mechanical assistance, from its original location on the Isle of Pines on Knife Lake in the heart of the Boundary Waters Canoe Area Wilderness. Here, from 1934 until her death in 1986, Dorothy lived a quiet life of service surrounded by nature's magnificence. As the Boundary Waters grew in popularity among canoeists, "The Root-beer Lady," as she became known, also sold homemade brew to many of the 6,000 visitors who paddled to her door each year (her guest books, dutifully signed by all visitors, are available for your perusal).

Walk through the simple rooms of her two cabins and view portions of an excellent documentary video about her life, and you may come to appreciate the many subtle things that make Dorothy's life remarkable. She evidently loved the long silences and solitary rigors of winter life at her island retreat, yet her summers were filled with enough uninvited visitors to make her one of the area's main tourist attractions. Without ever charging a fee, she used her training as a nurse to help wilderness travelers who were injured and sick. She even paid for an emergency float-plane evacuation for a man suffering from hypothermia whose party was unable to afford the flight. Perhaps that explains why an avalanche of signatures was easily gathered to petition the U.S. Forest Service to allow her to remain on her island home in the late 1970s when the Boundary Waters became closed to residents. Appropriately enough she was allowed the privilege of living out her days in the heart of canoe country.

The Dorothy Molter Museum is open weekends from her birthday, May 6, to Memorial Day each spring, then daily through September. Call (218) 827–3643 for more information and to make an appointment for visits outside normal hours.

Numerous resorts and outfitters in town can help even the most inexperienced adventurers gain access to the surrounding wilderness. Though the usual modes of travel in the BWCA are by canoe, skis, and snowshoes, explorers with more exotic tastes can arrange for kayak trips through **Piragis North Woods Company** (call toll-free 800–223–6565). In winter they can assume command at the helm of a sled-dog team under the guidance of polar explorer Paul Schurke at **Wintergreen Lodge** (call toll-free 800–584–9425).

Scandinavians have made a fascinating ritual of the sauna—a ritual that has elements both sacred and profane—and there is no better place to partake of its traditions than the ◆ **Ely Steam Bath.** For more than fifty years, work-worn loggers and miners, grimy from a day's labor in the area's once-great open-pit mines, have made the trek into town to catch up on local gossip, cleanse their bodies, and replenish their spirits in the steam bath's penetrating vapors. A visit to this humble landmark institution, found on Harvey Street near First Avenue, will have the same effects on you, as well as providing a unique window to one of Minnesota's most engaging off-the-beaten-path communities. The steam bath has separate public facilities for men and women, as well as smaller rooms available exclusively for couples. But for the full sociological experience, the public baths are the way to go. Typically the natives prolong their convivial ablutions by working up a sweat in the steam room, showering, and then sitting for a while in the antechamber to enjoy a cold drink before repeating the cycle a couple of more times. By their last visit to the steam room, the men are so well softened up that they often shave their gristly beards without need of shaving cream. Newcomers, however, may find themselves similarly poached after only one or two doses of Scandinavian heat.

Open for business Wednesday and Friday from 4:00 to 8:30 P.M. and on Saturdays from 2:00 to 8:30 P.M. year-round, the Ely Steam Bath boasts extremely modest prices. Towels are provided.

The Vermilion Iron Range, which runs south and west of Ely, is a small relative to the famous Mesabi Range farther west. But what it lacked in size, the Vermilion made up for in the purity of its ore and in its stature as the place where Minnesota's iron-ore rush began. The start of this world-class industrial bonanza was the ◆Soudan Underground Mine—the oldest, richest, and deepest mine in the state and now one of Minnesota's most fascinating tourist attractions.

Run by the Department of Natural Resources as a historic state park since mining operations ceased in 1962, the mine's several modest above-ground buildings and the 1924-vintage hoist (a huge cable, drum, and engine system that hauls loads up and down the Soudan's main shaft) are maintained in top working order. But instead of raising six-ton bins of dense reddish-brown hematite ore up to the surface every three to five minutes, as it has done for most of its working life, the hoist now transports rattling steel elevators, or "cages," full of visitors wearing hard hats.

After viewing a short film on the history of the Soudan, prepare yourself for a quick descent 2,341 feet below ground to level 27— the mine's deepest horizontal "drift," or passage, where the temperature year-round is a cool fifty degrees. The guide explains that the ride down will take three minutes traveling at about 10

135

miles per hour, but the dizzying blur of rock and steel visible through the elevator's single window gives the impression of much greater speed. The elevator finally comes to a noisy halt, the door opens, and a small train awaits to take you a quarter of a mile down a dark tunnel to a reconstructed mining site.

The reality of what it was like to work in such a place dawns on you slowly. Solitary mannequins placed far apart in a large cavern stand poised to drill holes with deafening, carbide-tipped, air-powered drills (the guide turns them on briefly). Under working conditions the headlamps that the miners wore were the only sources of light (other lights illuminating the scene are momentarily turned off so that you can appreciate the gloom), and a pervasive unhealthy dust frequently limited visibility even more. During lunch breaks and shift changes, the freshly drilled 10-foot-deep holes were filled with explosives, and the caverns were enlarged by blasting. Then, using heavy equipment, the laborers would load the ore into small railroad cars for the trip to the elevator. The best paid among the miners of this "Cadillac of underground mines" (conditions were considered excellent, and, with only thirteen deaths, the Soudan's safety record was very good) were the men who drilled and blasted the ceilings of vertical shafts that were up to 200 feet high. In 1962 each eight-hour shift that these men worked yielded a $24 wage.

If that sounds like no fun, consider the days before electricity and unionization brought their improvements. In the early 1890s, when the possibilities of open-pit mining at the Soudan site were exhausted and the enterprise went underground, miners wielded pickaxes for the duration of each twelve-hour shift. Illumination was cast by candles, one to a man. The mules that hauled the ore to the hoist stayed underground for six months at a time, and when they arrived at the surface for a well earned six-month vacation, their eyes were wrapped in layers of gauze that were removed gradually over the course of a week to prevent blindness.

Underground tours of the Soudan mine are offered daily for a modest fee throughout the summer; they leave the surface each half-hour and take about an hour. The interpretive film lasts ten minutes, there are above-ground exhibits in the information building, and the giant hoist can be seen in operation. Also, hiking trails lead to several of the Soudan's original open pits. For more information call toll-free within Minnesota (800) 652–9747; outside Minnesota (218) 753–2245.

Miners long ago discovered that nothing takes the chill off after a shift in the bowels of the earth than an authentic, home-cooked pasty—a delicious culinary tradition on the range that reflects the influence of immigrant Cornish miners. And the **Tower Bakery,** just a mile west of the Soudan Underground Mine on Minnesota 169 in the heart of Tower, has a reputation for some of the best pasties around. Park yourself at the counter, order a cup of coffee, and enjoy your vegetable, pork, and beef pie shaped like a half-moon. The crust is flaky, and the bill is so cheap that you may be inclined to buy a couple more for the road.

Detour about a dozen miles south of Tower on Highway 169 for an exploration of the Finnish heritage and architecture that characterizes much of the region's settlement history. **Sisu Heritage,** in the little town of Embarrass (occasionally noted for having the coldest temperature in the lower forty-eight states), provides visitors with two-hour guided tours of several preserved pioneer homesteads. The informative guides strike a balance between explaining subtle differences in log-building techniques developed by Finnish master builders and providing insights into cultural traditions, like the sauna, that were brought by the Finns to the northwoods. The tours are inexpensive and are offered during summer from Monday through Saturday. For reservations write Sisu Heritage, Inc., P.O. Box 127, Embarrass 55733.

Ice-hockey fans will want to pay a visit to a cube-shaped building on a prominent hill overlooking Route 53 in downtown Eveleth. The ◆ **United States Hockey Hall of Fame** stands as a tribute both to the sport and to the prominence it has enjoyed on the iron range since 1903, when the first game was played in Eveleth. Giants of the sport are immortalized in the Great Hall downstairs, where each star has his own pillar, plaque, and photograph. Upstairs a room dedicated to the U.S. Olympic hockey team contains special artifacts commemorating the gold-medal teams of 1960 and 1980. There is also a continually running video of the much-celebrated U.S. victory over the USSR in 1980.

A tunnellike exhibit with illustrations and audiotapes traces the history of hockey from its roots in 478 B.C. Other displays are dedicated to modern amateur, collegiate, and high school competition. If after all this adoration of the game you're itching to knock the puck around, you can do so at a mock shooting gallery wherein an electronic goalie defends a life-size goal from your best shots. The Hall of Fame is open year-round, seven days a week, except holidays, and charges a modest admission fee. For more information call (218) 744–5167.

As you're traveling west on Route 169 from Eveleth, you may notice that the landscape along both sides of the highway has a slightly unnatural appearance. There are trees, lakes, and occasionally rugged hills and valleys—just as you'd see elsewhere in northeastern Minnesota—but still, you think, something isn't quite right.

A visit to the interpretive center at ❖ **Ironworld USA** in Chisholm, 20 miles west of Eveleth, will clear up the mystery straight away, for at this fantastic historical museum, research library, and entertainment complex, which was completed in 1985 at a cost of $8.5 million, you'll learn that you've been traveling down the backbone of the Ojibway's Mesabi—the sleeping iron-ore giant. And the seventy-year endeavor to remove this creature from his resting place has left its mark on virtually everything in sight.

The spectacular views from Ironworld's several observation decks, historic trolley, and tourist railroad are typical. In all directions stands of second-growth timber mask flat-topped piles of discarded low-grade ore and other waste rock. And the lake you see at the bottom of a steeply terraced valley is actually an abandoned open-pit mine.

Ironworld USA, which was built to celebrate the special ethnic history of the iron range, will leave an indelible impression of the tremendous scope of Minnesota's iron-ore industry and the impact that it has had on the world. Wonderfully creative exhibits at the interpretive center chronicle the cultural traditions brought to the iron range by the masses of immigrants who came from all over Europe at the turn of the century. Everywhere in the building music and professionally crafted displays complement historic films and audiotapes of miners and their families describing their experiences. There are demonstrations of ethnic cooking and folk art traditions. Large exhibits bring to life the geological history of the area and the technology of taconite mining.

Meanwhile, outside there are regular ethnic music and dance performances in a beautifully landscaped garden. Food booths offer specialties that are traditional to the iron range's historic cultures.

Special concerts are held throughout summer in an acoustically superb, 1,600-seat outdoor amphitheater. Also a half-dozen festivals are held at Ironworld each year, drawing internationally renowned performers and musicians. Ironworld's entertainment areas and interpretive center are open daily from May through September for a small fee, whereas the research library, with its extensive genealogy archives, is open year-round. For more information write Ironworld USA, Box 392, Chisholm 55719 or call (218) 254–3321 or, toll-free from within Minnesota, (800) 372–6437.

Across Route 169 from Ironworld, on the edge of downtown Chisholm, the **Minnesota Museum of Mining** provides a slightly different perspective on the area's industrial history. Surrounding a building of rambling indoor exhibits, where a detailed scale model of a taconite processing plant is displayed prominently, are several monstrous steam shovels, a railroad engine, and an evolutionary progression of trucks that culminates in one of today's 127-ton behemoths. Nearby, a twenty-ton drag bucket, once used to scrape up car-sized chunks of Mesabi ore, rusts in isolation on the grass, only hinting at the size of the crane that was its companion. The museum is open daily from mid-May through September and charges a small fee. Call (218) 262–3895 for more information.

Travel a few more miles west along the iron range's forested moonscape and you'll arrive at Hibbing. Follow the signs at the northeast edge of town for the **Hull-Rust-Mahoning Mine overlook,** where you can watch gigantic trucks and cranes removing what ore remains in the world's largest open-pit iron mine. The pit yawns 2 miles across, 3 miles long, and more than 500 feet deep from the overlook interpretive center, where a short video and volunteer interpreters explain the operation. Blasting in the mine is frequently scheduled for Thursday mornings at 11:00 A.M.

Retracing your steps toward downtown Hibbing, you'll pass through a skeleton of a ghost town. A grid of streets flanked by sidewalks with weeds growing in the cracks and an occasional lamppost is all that's left of what was once a thriving mining settlement called, of all things, Hibbing. Like most communities on the iron range, Hibbing grew up on the edge of a mine. By 1918 industry managers determined that the town itself and all its inhabitants had to make way for the gaping pit that was to become the Hull-Rust-Mahoning Mine. The town site of Alice, 2 miles to the south, was selected as a suitable location for the transplanted population.

To make this move more palatable, the mining bosses built the town a high school that would match the immigrant miners' towering desire to better the lot of their children through education. Inexpensive tours of the fortresslike **Hibbing High School,** which was completed in 1923 at a cost of almost $4 million, are given Monday through Saturday throughout summer (call 218–263–3675 for more information). Among Hibbing High's most noted alumni is Bobby Zimmerman, a musically talented student now known to the world as Bob Dylan; Dylan's boyhood home, not open to the public, can be seen at 2425 Seventh Avenue South.

The state-of-the-art ◆**Paulucci Space Theatre** in Hibbing draws crowds year-round for mind-boggling multimedia programs on subjects that range from dinosaurs to outer space. Using a computer-driven arsenal of twenty-six slide projectors, a Spitz 512 Starball for stargazing, and a Cinema 360 fish-eye movie system that projects images all over the theater's domed ceiling, the Paulucci is among the top two-dozen planetariums in the nation. There is also an interesting gift shop. For information on the theater's inexpensive shows, call (218) 262–6720.

Cozy and hospitable accommodations in Hibbing can be found at the **Adams House bed-and-breakfast.** Marlene and Merrill Widmark, current owners of this 1927 English Tudor–style home, serve a continental breakfast and charge moderate rates. For reservations, write the Widmarks at 201 East Twenty-third Street, Hibbing 55746 or call (218) 263–9742.

Great Lakes shipping is the main economic force that put and has kept the city of Duluth on the map, and at this head-of-the-lakes international port, shipping primarily means iron ore. On any given day, spring through fall, there may be at anchor in the harbor several huge freighters from South America, Asia, or Europe. A good place to see them is from the breakwater that juts out into the lake from Canal Park, found at the south end of Canal Park Drive and next to Duluth's most famous landmark, the aerial lift bridge. Ocean-sized waves break against the shore, seagulls call stridently while winging overhead, and the exotic associations conjured up by the flags and foreign names on the ships can all conspire to transport your imagination far from the American heartland.

The ◈ **Canal Park Marine Museum,** which faces the park and the breakwater, is an excellent first stop if you want to learn more about Lake Superior and the global shipping industry that it supports. Upon entering the building you'll pass down a sloping hallway lined above and on the walls with weathered signs bearing the names of ships that once traveled the lakes. The lower floor has an auditorium that shows films about shipping and the Lake Superior environment several times daily. Large maps identify shipwreck sites and graphically depict the bottom contour of the world's largest freshwater lake. There are also exhibits on current underwater research projects and on the history of marine engine technology.

Upstairs three reconstructed staterooms, occupied by mannequins in period dress, convey a sense of what life below decks was like in the time of the Great Lakes steamer; also on display are numerous well-crafted models of historic ships. Another film-viewing area offers continually running shows on the U.S. Army Corps of Engineers, which operates the museum, and on the modern bulk-loading process for freighters. The information desk on the second floor will alert you to the origin of any ships moored in the harbor, and against the plate-glass windows facing the lake, telescopes are available for studying these big vessels. The museum is open year-round free of charge. For information about the arrival of ships in Duluth harbor, call (218) 727-2497.

Lake Superior Center is a second Duluth waterfront destination that provides insights into Lake Superior's preeminence among the world's freshwater resources. Though the exhibits at this new center, located at 353 Harbor Drive, are in the developmental stage, the vision that inspires it and its plans for the future are as sweeping as the lake at its door. A tour of the exhibits and a view of the center's multimedia show will inform you that Superior's cold, clear waters represent 20 percent of the fresh water on the earth's surface. You'll also gain an appreciation of the natural and cultural history of the lake and its watershed. Groups can arrange to explore the lake on three-hour ecology tours aboard a 63-foot research vessel.

Parallels with Lake Baikal in Siberia, with which the center has established a sister-lake relationship, are creatively displayed through several exhibits. Dedicated to public education concerning the lake and the importance of freshwater resources, Lake Superior Center is raising money for a new $28 million facility, replete with a 180,000-gallon aquarium, scheduled for opening in 1995. Until then the center will be open daily during summer, free of charge. For information about programs call (218) 720–3033.

Just west of Canal Park, in a slip beside Harbor Drive, sits proudly the 610-foot freighter **SS *William A. Irvin*.** From 1938 to 1978 this steam-powered vessel served as the flagship of the U.S. Steel Company fleet, the largest flotilla of ore carriers in the world. During summer excellent forty-five-minute guided tours that range from stem to stern are conducted, for a modest fee, many times daily.

The sheer mass of the *Irvin* can hardly escape your notice as you enter the gigantic middle hold through a door at the top of the gangplank. But somehow it's through the smaller details of the ship's construction that the *Irvin*'s incredible size is driven home. After climbing and descending several of the sixteen steep stair-cases encountered during the tour, you find yourself outside the engine room on the stern deck. The links of a chain, supporting a three-ton emergency anchor nearby, weigh forty pounds each. A mooring rope coiled at your feet is almost as thick as your trunk.

To get this ship up to speed with its 14,000-ton load (11 knots was tops, 13 when running "light"), it took two 1,000-horse-power engines burning a ton of coal per hour. It also took a lot of hard work and sweat. Even in Lake Superior's cool climate, temperatures in the engine room while the ship was under way ranged from 100 to 115 degrees, with 93 percent humidity. In balmy Detroit temperatures were 115 to 130 degrees, and the poor guys stoking the boiler had to contend with a scalding 200 degrees. Above 115 degrees, the guide explains, everyone had to wear gloves to keep from getting burned when handling the brass equipment.

It was an entirely different kind of trip for the *Irvin*'s VIP passengers in their wood-paneled staterooms at the other end of the ship. Daily activities for these major stockbrokers and U.S. Steel clients included trapshooting, driving golf balls into the lake, playing shuffleboard, and participating in an occasional game of baseball in an empty hold. Gourmet meals were prepared by a special chef and served in an elegant dining room following cocktails in the guests' private lounge. For a schedule of tours of the *Irvin,* call (218) 722–5573.

An enjoyable way to see Duluth's waterfront is aboard the **North Shore Scenic Railroad.** Day trips range in length from one and one-half hours (Lester River) to six hours (Two Harbors) and are fully narrated, providing you with a bevy of information about the Duluth area. You'll learn about everything from how the port was built to how to keep the seagulls away from your window at the Edgewater Motel.

In the evenings you can ride the Dinner Train, which features three different menus: Elegance and Romance, Buffet Dinner, and Pizza Train. The Scenic Railroad departs from the historic Depot building, 506 West Michigan Street. Call (218) 722–1273 for more information.

The tremendous wealth resulting from the burgeoning success of the iron-ore industry at the turn of the century is evident in two Duluth estates along the Lake Superior shoreline on stately London Road, east of downtown. **Glensheen,** an elegant, thirty-nine-room, Jacobean-style manor house set in a seven-acre wooded glen, has become one of Duluth's most popular attractions. Since assuming ownership from the Congdon family in 1968, the University of Minnesota, Duluth, has been conducting tours that focus on Glensheen's outstanding architecture, extensive hand-crafted woodwork, and furnishings that date back to 1908, when the estate was completed. Glensheen, located at 3200 London Road, is also available for rental. For information on rentals and for schedules of the inexpensive tours (reservations are recommended), call (218) 724–8864.

A slightly more intimate way to partake in Duluth's opulent past is to let a room for the night at **The Mansion,** a twenty-five-room bed-and-breakfast estate situated a half-mile down the road from Glensheen. Built between 1928 and 1932 for Marjorie Congdon Dudley (the daughter of Chester A. Congdon, master of Glensheen) and her husband, Harry C. Dudley, a mining engineer, The Mansion has seven acres of wooded grounds and more than 500 feet of secluded Lake Superior shoreline. There are ten guest rooms in all, three in the former maids' quarters (which are moderately priced), five in the main part of the house, and an apartment that rents for a two-night minimum stay (moderately to expensively priced). All guests can enjoy the beautiful screened porch, the spacious living room, the upstairs den, and a library with a fireplace and lovely hand-carved-oak built-in bookcases lined with leather-bound volumes. A large country breakfast is served. For reservations write The Mansion, 3600 London Road, Duluth 55804 or call (218) 724–0739.

Another more diminutive, but hardly less luxurious, Duluth bed-and-breakfast is the **Barnum House.** Built by businessman and philanthropist George Barnum in 1910, this 8,000-square-foot house was originally designed to showcase an extensive collection of fine arts and accommodate frequent guests. It still does.

Current owners/innkeepers Dick and Dorothy Humes, who raised their family in the house before turning it into a bed-and-breakfast in 1991, have gone to great lengths to maintain the original opulence of this grand mansion. From the glass-enclosed veranda by the front door to the cozy sitting room with its unique arched fireplace, the entire downstairs area has a warm, friendly feeling. The five upstairs guest rooms each have their own distinct character. Two, the Barnum Suite and the Humes Suite, have working fireplaces. Three have access to a veranda overlooking a nearby ravine and brook. All rooms are appointed with beautiful antique furnishings, queen- or king-size beds, and private baths. To make reservations call or write well in advance to Barnum House Bed & Breakfast, 2211 East Third Street, Duluth 55812 or call toll-free (800) 879–5437.

Duluth's historic train station, a striking 1892 châteauesque structure with steep-roofed towers and a great-hall with a high cathedral ceiling, is several destinations in one. A permanent collection of paintings by Eastman Johnson is a cornerstone of **the Depot**'s several art galleries. Eastman, who was America's most celebrated artist of the middle nineteenth century, lived and painted in the Duluth area for two years. As the displayed paintings and drawings indicate, he enjoyed producing portraits of presidents, as well as of the Ojibway Indians he found on the Minnesota frontier. Also on display are exhibits on logging history and Norwegian wood carving.

A train museum in the boarding-platform area of the Depot features Minnesota's first steam engine, on display next to one of the largest locomotives in the world—the Mallet Number 227, which burned ten to twelve tons of coal *per hour* while hauling more than a hundred iron-ore cars from Tower to the docks in

Duluth harbor. Surrounding the tracks is a boardwalk with reconstructed Duluth storefronts circa 1910.

The historic Depot building is adjacent to Duluth's **Depot Theatre,** where ballet and theater performances and symphony orchestra concerts are held. The exhibit areas in the Depot, which is located at 506 West Michigan Street, are open daily for a modest fee. For information on special programs, such as the annual All American Railroad Days celebration each July, call (218) 727–8025.

History buffs with a taste for documents have an interesting time at the **Karpeles Manuscript Library Museum,** 902 East First Street. Founded by Dave Karpeles to "renew the sense of purpose our children are missing," this museum is a decidedly eclectic assemblage of historic documents and manuscripts. You'll find a page from Noah Webster's original dictionary and a stanza from Mozart's *Marriage of Figaro.* There's even a gas bill paid by Thomas Edison (suppose the rates hastened the invention of the light bulb?). The list goes on and on, with each display seemingly as random as the next. Little historical background is given regarding any of the documents in the exhibit itself, but brochures with additional information about each piece are available near the entryway. The museum is open daily year-round and is free. Call (218) 728–0630 for more information.

Lovers of old stadiums and baseball played on real grass should make it a point to see the Duluth-Superior Dukes. In days of old the Dukes were a Detroit Tigers farm team, and future stars such as Gates Brown and Denny McLain used the grounds of historic Wade Stadium, built in 1941, to learn their craft. Today the Dukes are one of six franchises in the independent Northern League (St. Paul, Sioux City, Sioux Falls, Thunder Bay, and Winnipeg are the others). The baseball is not quite of major-league caliber, but neither are the prices—a family of four can get tickets, a hot dog, and a soft drink for less than $25. Best of all, the games are a lot of fun. Call Dukes Baseball at (218) 727–4525 for schedule and ticket information.

Though it's difficult to do, if you're passing through Duluth in autumn and can take your eyes off the oceanlike sweep of Lake Superior and the spectacular fall foliage along the shore, look skyward—you may well see something striking. Better yet, find your way to ◆**Hawk Ridge** atop the string of hills behind the city, because regardless of which direction you may be traveling, tens of thousands of hawks, eagles, and falcons will be winging their way overhead in their annual fall migration. And this small nature preserve, dedicated to observing and recording this singular event, offers what some say is the best viewing site in the country.

There are several observation posts at Hawk Ridge, each oriented to a different wind direction, as well as a network of hiking trails and a bird-banding station. Volunteer naturalists on duty daily from mid-August through November can assist you in the fine art of distinguishing between the various species. On a good day—one with clear skies and a wind from the west or northwest, creating updrafts upon which the grand birds can soar effortlessly about—you may see thousands of these beautiful winged predators. More than 30,000 sightings of individual birds of the same species have been recorded in a single twelve-hour period during the peak flyover time, which is usually mid-September.

Hawk Ridge is located along the Skyway Parkway, just north of the intersection of Glenwood Avenue and Forty-third Avenue East. Admission is free, though donations for the support of the reserve are encouraged.

Each summer Duluth hosts two cultural events that attract visitors from throughout the region. The **Blues Festival,** held annually over a weekend in early August, attracts major entertainers from around the country. A week later the **Port of Duluth Festival** features (along with concerts, jet-ski races, and other happenings) tours of selected U.S. Coast Guard ships and giant wooden sailing ships, like the 179-foot HMS *Rose,* a replica of a British frigate that fought against the Blue Coats in New York harbor during the Revolutionary War. For more information on these events, call the Duluth Convention and Visitors Bureau, toll-free, at (800) 4–DULUTH.

Duluth's annual **Winter Sports Festival** in January brings several other sorts of thrill seekers out of hiding. Competitors from all over North America come to Duluth for the grueling 500-mile John Beargrease Sled Dog Marathon, which runs around the clock for four consecutive days. Large teams of powerful dogs driven by hardy mushers travel an old winter mail route from Duluth to Grand Portage and back. Not far behind them is a pack of snowmobile racers who buzz through town on their way from Thunder Bay, Ontario, to the outskirts of the Twin Cities. There are snowshoe races, and, moving at a more soothing pace, a

HMS *Rose*, at Port of Duluth Festival

parade of antique horse-drawn cutters. For more information on these events, call the Duluth Convention and Visitors Bureau toll-free at (800) 438–5884.

LAKE COUNTY

As you leave Duluth driving northeast on Route 61, you enter an enchanted realm. For 150 miles the North Shore Scenic Drive hugs close to the rocky, wooded, mountain-lined rim of the world's largest freshwater sea. Although there's no hint of salt in the offshore breezes and there are no tides, in almost all other respects the cold, clear water stretching blue and silver to the horizon may as well be an ocean. The moods of Superior—from its furious northeasters in late autumn to the infinite calm of August's doldrums—are just too grand to belong to a lake. The shoreline cliffs were built to the same larger-than-life scale. Even the mammoth ocean-bound freighters, which at night look like distant sparkling cities adrift beneath the stars, are dwarfed by the magnificence of this mere "lake."

To help get yourself properly acclimated to the North Shore's maritime environment, a couple of shops in Knife River will fix you up with a supply of fish lured from Superior's depths. Depending on the month and the day's catch, **Mel's Fish** and **Russ Kendall's Smokehouse**—both located along Scenic Drive—carry smoked or fresh lake trout, whitefish, herring, and salmon.

Next stop is Two Harbors, whose two natural bays became an early locale for iron-ore shipping. As the staff and volunteers can tell you at the **Lake County Historical Society museum,** which overlooks the huge ore docks from the corner of Waterfront Drive and South Avenue, Minnesota's first minuscule shipment of iron ore traveled from the Tower-Soudan mine in St. Louis County to Two Harbors in 1884. The amount of ore that passed through town that entire year—some 60,000 tons—can today be carried by a single ship.

A short walk toward the lake from the museum leads to the permanent docking site of the *Edna G,* an extremely long-lived, coal-fired tugboat that was in service at the docks from 1896 until the early 1980s, when freighters finally became capable of precise maneuvering in such small spaces as Agate Bay. The boat landing and breakwater at Lighthouse Point are good sites for watching these big ships dock and load. The museum staff can tell you which ships are coming and when.

Now then, let's say you have a question about sandpaper that's keeping you awake at night. Well, breathe a sigh of relief, because at Two Harbors's **Dawn Museum,** which contains the world's largest sandpaper exhibit, answers to your most perplexing queries about abrasives are likely to be found. This one-of-a-kind museum occupies the former office of John Dawn, a Two Harbors lawyer who in 1902 became the first secretary of an obscure company called Minnesota Mining and Manufacturing—today known the world over as 3M.

The first of the museum's two rooms gives a brief history of 3M from its formation until 1919, when company headquarters were moved from Two Harbors to St. Paul. An interesting display charts the company's growth and shows early models of some of its most famous products, including Scotch Tape and Post-it Notes. A portion of the second room documents changes in the company's logo through the years. But most of the space is devoted to that most handy abrasive material, sandpaper. For example, did you know that a very fine sandpaper is used to polish optical lenses? And that dentists use waterproof sandpaper to polish your teeth? And that 3M manufactures more than fifty million different sandpaper products for its customers around the world? For this and more impressive information, visit the Dawn Museum at 508 Second Avenue. Admission is inexpensive, and the doors are open daily in summer and on weekends through the rest of the year.

Another Two Harbors Museum, the **Great Lakes Fur Trade Museum and Gift Shoppes,** features an eclectic assortment of objects and artifacts collected from the age of the voyageurs. An original Hudson Bay blanket, measuring 15 by 6 feet, hangs beside a collection of cookery made by Miles Standish, a blacksmith and direct descendent of his Puritan namesake. A "Vice Exhibit" documents tobacco and alcohol products of the time. And if reviewing this material gives rise to questions, owners Wad and Caroline Miller, both experts on the subject of the fur trade, will gladly regale you with spirited answers. The museum, at 112 Waterfront Drive, is open daily, free of charge.

At the mouth of the Stewart River, about 3 miles northeast of Two Harbors, one of the North Shore's best-known eateries attracts travelers with its international reputation (Canada, after all, is only a couple of hours away). The homemade baked goods at **Betty's Pies** are indeed delicious. Good inexpensive sandwiches and made-from-scratch soups are served, too.

You'll notice the landscape taking a turn for the dramatic just up the shore from Betty's as you approach the entrance to the newly completed Silver Creek Tunnel. Beside the entrance you can browse through the locally made crafts at **Pioneer Crafts Coop**. From here to Thunder Bay precipitous shoreline cliffs and awesome waterfalls are regular roadside attractions.

Because of the dangers posed by this inhospitable coast, the movers and shakers of the steel industry persuaded Congress to build the ◆**Split Rock Lighthouse** in 1909. This plan was developed following a treacherous storm in November 1905, in which thirty ships were damaged or sunk, including two in the immediate vicinity of a prominent cliff located 20 miles northeast of Two Harbors. The Minnesota Historical Society now runs the site; and, as its guides will tell you, getting U.S. taxpayers to fund the lighthouse was in fact a maneuver that enabled the steel barons to avoid having to institute costly safety procedures.

A beautiful interpretive center with an excellent film and exhibits complements the hour-long tour of the well-preserved light and the light-keepers' residences (there were a head keeper and two assistants with families). The experience provides yet another perspective on the iron-ore industry that has been so essential to Minnesota's livelihood. It also illuminates what life was like on Superior's shores in the early decades of this century for local residents and for the employees of the strictly regimented and now-extinct U.S. Lighthouse Service.

During the construction of the lighthouse, which required the assembly of a steam-powered derrick to hoist workers and materials up the 100-foot cliff face, Split Rock was accessible only by lake. Soon after the North Shore highway was completed in 1924, however, the facility became the most visited lightstation in the country. By 1969 the sophistication of navigational equipment had rendered obsolete the ten-second-interval beacon and foghorn (which were detectable more than 20 and 5 miles away, respectively), and Split Rock was deeded to the state.

The Split Rock Interpretive Center, Route 61, is open weekends in winter and daily through summer months, whereas tours of the lightstation are offered only from mid-May through mid-October. A small fee is charged and an inexpensive state park sticker is required for admission. For more information call (218) 226–3065.

A view of the lake that surpasses even the one from the top of the Split Rock tower (itself 167 feet above the lake level) can be found about 12 miles farther up the shore. Just after passing the Palisade Baptist Church on the lake side of Route 61, you'll see an unmarked wayside parking area on the same side of the highway with a narrow, winding road leading out of sight up a steep embankment. This road leads to the top of **Palisade Head,** a spectacular 200-foot promontory that presents a vertical face to the lake and that in summer is a popular playground for rock climbers. If you tire of watching men and women cheating death on the cliff, you can also look for a nesting pair of rare peregrines—falcons famous for attacking their prey in midflight—that have recently claimed this precipitous environment as a summer home. Also, the ground cover on top of Palisade Head offers outstanding blueberry picking in mid-to-late summer.

As grand as the views from Palisade Head may be, if you really want to take your measure against the North Shore's hills, you should spend some time on the new **Superior Hiking Trail.** The rugged trail at present winds from Castle Danger to Grand Marais, connecting eight state parks in the process. Scenic overlooks punctuate the trail, as do occasional campsites (equipped with pit toilets and fire rings) and road crossings. The trail is designed so that hikers can set out for just a few hours or hike for days. When the many, many hours of volunteer labor that have been undertaken to make the trail are complete, the Lake Superior Hiking Trail will run the full distance from Duluth to the Canadian border. Trail maps are available free of charge at ranger stations and tourist information centers all along the shore.

Minnesota Highway 1's winding 60-mile journey from Illgen City on the Superior shore to Ely is one of those Arrowhead roads that continually draw your attention out the window to witness tall stands of virgin timber, sparkling lakes and rivers, and moose and deer that momentarily break from their foraging to give you a mildly curious look. A little more than halfway along its length, this highway is intersected by Lake County Road 2, very near the location of one of Minnesota's most unusual learning centers: the ◆ **Great Lakes School of Log Building.**

Since 1974, Ron Brodigan has been teaching experientially oriented courses in the basics of log construction for folks who've always dreamed of living in their own house made of trees. During the fourteen-day classes, students actually build a log structure such as the many that occupy the rustic school site (accommodations are in wood-heated bunkhouses, bathing is done in traditional Finnish saunas and solar showers, and participants provide their own food). At the end of each course, students with no previous construction experience or special strength return home with the necessary skills to undertake their own projects. Ron also offers rural-skills short courses that concern various aspects of living in the backcountry. Per-day fees at the school are inexpensive. To register or to receive more information, write the school at 570 County Road 2, Isabella 55607 or call (218) 365–2126 (evenings) or (612) 822–5955 (days).

COOK COUNTY

If you're driving up the shore at a pace that's suitable for taking in all there is to see and do, by now you may well have happily consumed all the fish that you purchased back in Knife River. No matter—in the tiny community of Schroeder you can stop by the **Cross River General Store,** where butcher Bill Jordan proffers an impressive assortment of homemade sausages in a freezer next to his "Cadillac of pizzas." Among the twenty-one different sausages that Bill produces, only a few are likely to be household names. Many of the rest—Ukrainian, Swedish potato, Spanish, Mexican, Italian, Polynesian (with pineapple), and Belgian *tripp*—might be appropriate for a United Nations picnic. There are also sausages that draw their inspiration from sources closer to home, such as those made of lake trout, wild rice (available with pork or turkey), and porketta (an iron-range tradition). Then, Bill says with a sparkle in his eye, there are the others—like jungle sausage, with bananas and teriyaki, and Hobbit sausage, made with rutabaga. *Bon appetit!*

Five miles farther along the highway, you'll cross the Temperance River, which at this elevation flows within the borders of **Temperance River State Park.** Some sources say this stream received its name in playful recognition of the fact that it was one of the few North Shore waterways without a sandbar at its mouth. Also, among the many rivers along the shore that have impressive waterfalls—such as the Gooseberry, Baptism, and Cascade—the Temperance is distinguished for having carved a fantastic series of caldrons and spillways through the lava bedrock formation on the upstream side of the highway. A short trail winds along the section of the river, beginning from the parking area near the highway bridge.

Grand Marais is a focal point of North Shore recreational activity winter and summer. It is also a quaint coastal town in its own right, with a history steeped in fishing and logging traditions. When you are entering the community from the southwest, visible to your right is Grand Marais's harbor, where you'll find the North Shore's only sailboat charter and instruction center outside of Duluth. **Northwind Sailing** offers short rides (prices are inexpensive for groups of four to six), classes in basic and advanced sailing, harbor cruises in a 26-foot motor launch, and a captained or bareboat sailboat-charter service. For more information write Northwind Sailing, Grand Marais Harbor, Box 973, Grand Marais 55604 or call (218) 387–1265.

Adventuresome souls who would prefer to explore the Grand Marais shoreline by sea-kayak can rent these comfortable and surprisingly stable vessels for a nominal fee, either by the hour or by the day, from **Superior Kayaks.** Brad Ranning usually has his kayaks on display at the north end of the harbor; otherwise, he can be reached at (218) 387–2605.

Grand Marais's first bed-and-breakfast establishment, **Pincushion Mountain Bed and Breakfast,** is perched atop the ridge overlooking town 3 miles up the Gunflint Trail. With 15 miles of groomed and tracked trails beginning outside its door, Pincushion is perfect for cross-country skiers in winter and for hikers (the Superior Hiking Trail is also nearby) and mountain-bike enthusiasts the rest of the year; lodge-to-lodge skiing, hiking, or biking can be arranged. The B&B is also a comfortable place to stay even if you aren't looking for such an active getaway. Scott and Mary Beattie are gracious hosts, offering their guests comfortable, modern rooms, outstanding full breakfasts, and a warm family atmosphere, all at moderate rates. For reservations write Pincushion Mountain Bed and Breakfast, Box 181, Grand Marais 55604 or call (218) 387–1276 or, toll-free from within Minnesota, (800) 542–1226.

Grand Marais's wilderness highway—the Gunflint Trail—is another Arrowhead road deserving of all the historic and romantic associations brought to mind by its name. Originally no more than an Indian footpath, the road today meanders between lakeshores and climbs up and over steep rocky ridges for 53 miles before suddenly dispersing like a river delta into a network of boat landings along the shores of Canadian-border Lake Saganaga. The Gunflint has numerous jumping-off points to the Boundary Waters Canoe Area, which borders the trail for half its length. (Boundary Waters travel information is available at the Superior National Forest ranger stations in Tofte and Grand Marais. Wilderness travel permits can be obtained by writing **BWCA Reservations,** Superior National Forest, Box 338, Duluth 55801 or by calling 218–720–5440.)

There are plenty of resorts and outfitters along the Gunflint, too, the latter providing equipment, food, and route-planning services for those interested in canoeing the BWCA's pristine waters (write the **Gunflint Trail Association,** 434 Gunflint Trail, Grand Marais 55604 or call toll-free 800–338–6932 for a list of outfitters and resorts and for hiking, biking, and skiing information). Come winter, the Gunflint has several outstanding networks of snowmobile and cross-country–skiing trails, including one that provides skiers with access to a most unusual type of accommodation: the yurt.

For centuries the people of the Mongolian plateaus have found cylindrical, peak-roofed tents, or yurts, to be convivial places to spend the night. Yurts are also much warmer than standard tents when outfitted with a woodstove, which they accommodate quite easily. Ted and Barbara Young of ◆**Boundary Country Trekking** have established three of these dwellings an easy day's ski apart along the Banadad Trail. Each of the one-room, canvas-covered yurts sleeps four to six, with accoutrements that include bunk beds, skylights, woodstoves, and an outhouse nearby.

You can either ski from yurt to yurt or to a recently built backwoods cabin reachable only on skis. The Youngs cheerfully shuttle your gear to the following day's destination and upon your arrival prepare outstanding meals, including such specialties as roast duck, grilled trout, and the almost-mystical Mongolian firepot dinner. Two lodges at either end of the Banadad Trail provide more civilized surroundings, or if yurts are too luxurious for your tastes, guided ski trips into the wilderness with dogsled support can be arranged. Prices for the yurt-to-yurt program are expensive, though they include three meals per day, lodging, and shuttle. For more information write Boundary Country Trekking, Gunflint Trail 67–1, Grand Marais 55604 or call toll-free (800) 322–8327. Another destination along the Gunflint Trail that's well worth the effort required to reach it is the 3.5-mile hike that will take you to the top of Minnesota's highest peak. You'll find the ✦ **Eagle Mountain** trailhead 17 miles northwest of Grand Marais, at the junction of Superior National Forest Roads 153 and 158 (the Gunflint and Tofte ranger stations have maps). Throughout its length the trail winds through such dense forest that you really haven't a clue as to where you are. Then suddenly the sky opens up and you find yourself on the edge of a dramatic escarpment 2,301 feet above sea level that provides a sweeping view of the forested wilderness to the south, west, and north. It is a truly magical place to be during evening light, when the surfaces of a half-dozen lakes down below are set on fire— though make sure you bring a flashlight, as the hike back to the car is a nasty one in the dark.

The lure of the North Shore for those seeking a place to revel in nature's glories is not a new phenomenon. As soon as the highway was completed from Duluth to Fort William and Port Arthur (now Thunder Bay) in 1924, the Superior shoreline quickly became a popular destination for the touring crowd. It even attracted the mighty Babe Ruth, boxer Jack Dempsey, and writer Ring Lardner, who were part of a group that banded together to build an exclusive wilderness retreat near Hovland called ✦ **Naniboujou Lodge.** But perhaps the establishment's namesake—a mythological trickster of the North American woodland Indian cultures—was a poor choice, for the project ground to a halt following the stock market crash of 1929, with only the main lodge and dining room completed.

Today Naniboujou's moderately priced rooms attract guests who come to collect agates on the beach or hike, ski, and fish beside the Brule River in the adjacent **Judge C. R. Magney State Park.** The dining room has an even larger clientele drawn by the very good fresh fish and poultry dishes (among others) and the fresh-baked breads and desserts served by owners Tim and Nancy Ramey. The setting for these moderately priced repasts is a large room whose lofty ceiling was painted in the 1920s with a bold, colorful motif inspired by Cree Indian mythology. Ornate paper chandeliers hang above. The huge fireplace at one end consists of more than 200 tons of native rock. Outside, the building's wood-shingled exterior blends nicely with the sprawling grounds that stretch down to the lakeshore. For more information write Naniboujou Lodge, HC–1, Box 505, Grand Marais 55604 or call (218) 387–2688.

The last 20 miles of Minnesota's Lake Superior shoreline take you through the Ojibway-owned Grand Portage Indian Reservation, one of the most historically significant and beautiful areas in all of Minnesota. After topping a steady incline that builds for several miles, Route 61 suddenly crests at a wayside parking area with a dramatic view of Grand Portage's large natural harbor and the Susie Island chain beyond. On a clear day you can also see Michigan's Isle Royale National Park in the hazy distance. Rising up from the shore is a steep escarpment of hills, over which hardy voyageurs during the latter part of the eighteenth century carried their heavy birchbark canoes and many tons of animal pelts tied in ninety-pound bundles.

The white-cedar stockade and log buildings at ✦ **Grand Portage National Monument** have been painstakingly reconstructed by the National Park Service to preserve the spirit of this hub of the fur trade. Costumed guides and special events like the annual Rendezvous and Powwow in mid-August give visitors a vivid impression of the life-style that reigned here from 1784 to 1803, when the North West Company used the settlement as the headquarters of its fur trade empire. Each summer hundreds of voyageurs, portaging their canoes and bearing backbreaking loads of furs from their wintering posts in the Canadian Northwest, hiked down the 9-mile Grand Portage trail. They were met at the stockade by their counterparts, who had traveled by even-larger birchbark freight canoes across the Great Lakes from Montreal with heavy supplies of trade goods. For several weeks in midsummer, the two groups exchanged their cargoes and, with the help of local Ojibway, celebrated one of the biggest parties on the frontier. Leaving enough time to return safely to their respective wintering posts, the two groups then loaded up their canoes for the long trip home. The monument, which is well marked along Route 61, is open daily from mid-May to mid-October for a small fee. For information on special programs, call (218) 387–2788.

The dock in front of the Grand Portage monument welcomes ships from the open lake, just as it did hundreds of years ago. Throughout summer it is also the dock site of the passenger ferry *Wenonah,* which departs daily for the nearest end of Michigan's **Isle Royale National Park,** 22 miles offshore; round-trip voyages on this ferry last most of the day and are expensive. Those wishing to circumnavigate this largest island in the largest lake in the world can book passage on the *Voyageur,* which departs every other day from a landing at the northeast end of the harbor. For more information about these excursions, write the Grand Portage–Isle Royale Transportation Lines, 1507 North First Street, Superior, WI 54880 or call (715) 392–2100.

You'll understand why the voyageurs preferred a 9-mile hike through the mosquito-infested woods to a canoe trip down the Pigeon River, which forms the Minnesota-Ontario border, if you pay a visit to ◈ **Grand Portage State Park.** This newest of Minnesota's state parks provides parking and an access trail to 120-foot High Falls on the Pigeon River, Minnesota's highest waterfall. To find it follow Route 61 almost to its terminus at the U.S. Customs station, where there is a small parking lot on the north side of the road.

Like the voyageurs before them, the loggers who worked the Pigeon River valley around the turn of the century were also intimidated by High Falls. Through the mist you can see the remains of a flume that carried their logs past the waterfall without the logs being turned into splinters. Still, the river's many violent rapids were so rough that a specially low grade of lumber was developed to market boards made from Pigeon River logs.

ACKNOWLEDGMENTS

Writing and revising this book has been a team effort. For the original research, special thanks are due the Minnesota Office of Tourism, the Minnesota Historical Society, and convention and visitors bureau staff in Rochester, Winona, Mankato, Northfield, Owatonna, Austin, Worthington, Alexandria, Thief River Falls, Moorhead, Grand Rapids, and St. Cloud. Also, Shotsy Johnson; Joan, Jeanne, and Gordy Shepard; Scot Hunter; and Libby Aurand provided invaluable research assistance.

The third edition has benefited greatly from Trip Johnson's creative enthusiasm. It was he who, this time around, ventured Minnesota's backroads to document most of the new additions. And to Suzanne, whose many dozens of phone calls have ensured that the book's information is timely, I owe a huge and loving thanks.

Index

159

Pincushion Mountain Bed and Breakfast, 153
Pioneer Crafts Coop, 150
Pipestone National Monument, 79–80
Piragis North Woods Company, 134
Plains Art Museum, 95
Planes of Fame War Birds Air Museum, 18–19
Polish Museum, 32
Port of Duluth Festival, 146
Pottery Place, 23
Pottery Salesroom, 23
powwow, Lower Sioux Agency, 63
Pride of Rainy Lake, 128–29

R
Ramsey Mill, 13
Rapid River Logging Camp, 113
Red Gables Inn, 25
Red Lake River, 97
Redwing Stoneware Co., 23
Redwood County Museum, 60
Rice County Courthouse, 45
Riverside Farm and Studio, 75
Rollag Store, 90
Root River Canoe Route, 35
Root River State Trail, 35–36
Runestone Museum, 84
Russian Piroshki and Teahouse, 7–8
Russ Kendall's Smokehouse, 148

S
Scanlan House, The, 36
Scenic Valley Winery, 36
Schech's Mill, 41
Schell Brewery, 65
Schumacher's New Prague Hotel, 69–70

Seppmann Windmill, 74
Shetek Revisited, 82
Sibley House, 11
Sinclair Lewis Boyhood Home, 107
Sinclair Lewis Interpretive Center, 106
Sisu Heritage, 137
Soo Pass Ranch, 95
Soudan Underground Mine, 135–37
Southeastern Minnesota Forest Resource Center, 36–37
Spicer Castle, 56–57
Split Rock Lighthouse, 150–51
SS *William A. Irvin*, 142–43
Steam Engine Days, 40
Steam Engine Museum, 40–41
Stearns County Heritage Center, 103–4
St. James Hotel, 22–23
St. John's Abbey and University Church, 105–6
St. Paul City Hall and Ramsey County Courthouse, 6–7
St. Paul Gangster Tours, 6
St. Paul Saints, 10
St. Paul YMCA Camp du Nord, 131
St. Peter Regional Treatment Center, 68
Summer Folk Festival, 90
Superior Hiking Trail, 151
Superior Kayaks, 153
Superior National Forest ranger station, Grand Marais, 154
Superior National Forest ranger station, Tofte, 154
Superior Whitewater, 121–22
Susie Island chain, 156

HISTORIC SITES

MUSEUMS

About the Author

Born in St. Paul, John Shepard has written extensively about his home state. He writes and reads essays for Minnesota Public Radio and writes and produces educational videos on outdoor recreation and the environment for the home market. He remains a contributing editor to *Canoe* magazine and has freelanced for *Cross County Skier,* the *St. Paul Pioneer Press Dispatch,* and *Minneapolis-St. Paul* magazine. His articles have appeared in the *New York Daily News, Los Angeles Times, Detroit News,* and *Baltimore Sun.*